CRUMBLING FOUNDATIONS

Books by Donald G. Bloesch

CRUMBLING FOUNDATIONS

Death and Rebirth in an Age of Upheaval

Donald G. Bloesch

Academie Books Grand Rapids, Michigan
Zondervan Publishing House

CRUMBLING FOUNDATIONS
Copyright © 1984 by The Zondervan Corporation
Grand Rapids, Michigan

ACADEMIE BOOKS is an imprint of Zondervan Publishing House,
1415 Lake Drive, S.E., Grand Rapids, Michigan 49506.

Library of Congress Cataloging in Publication Data

Bloesch, Donald G., 1928–
    Crumbling foundations
    Bibliography: p.
    Includes indexes
    1. Church renewal.   2. Evangelicalism.   3. Christianity
–20th century.   4. Moral conditions.   I. Title.
BV600.2.B565   1984   270.8'28   84-13173
ISBN 0-310-29821-0

Designed by Louise Bauer

Printed in the United States of America

85 86 87 88 89 / 10 9 8 7 6 5 4 3 2

To
Arlo Duba,
Dean of Dubuque Theological Seminary

If God did not exist, everything would be permitted.

FEODOR DOSTOEVSKY

We shall be ineffective and harmless unless we realize that naked paganism has burst forth again and we must recover the real meaning of Christianity.

FLORENCE ALLSHORN

It is beginning to look as though there is a worldwide fundamental conflict between Christianity and the modern state—a conflict which has little to do with whether the state espouses a leftist or rightist political philosophy.

PAUL VITZ

In these days of the world's agony, we feel keenly that we are living in a fallen world, torn asunder by incurable contradictions. And it is most notable that this sense of the world's fallen state is accompanied not by an increased, but by a decreased sense of sin.

NICHOLAS BERDYAEV

Contents

Abbreviations

RSV	Revised Standard Version
NEB	New English Bible
NIV	New International Version
NKJV	New King James Version

Acknowledgments

I want to acknowledge the solid help I have received from my wife, Brenda, especially in the areas of research and copy-editing. I also wish to thank Peg Saunders, faculty secretary at Dubuque Theological Seminary, for her careful typing of this manuscript. In addition, I am grateful to James Gingery and Mary Anne Knefel, reference librarians at our seminary; to Richard Mouw of Fuller Theological Seminary for providing data on the Netherlands; to Keith Roderick of the Society of St. Stephen for information on Russian Christians; and to Arthur Cochrane, from whom I have learned much concerning the church struggle in Nazi Germany.

Preface

I have been led to write this book to fortify my fellow Christians in the ever-growing struggle to maintain the integrity of the church's witness in a time when the moral and spiritual foundations of Western culture are collapsing. The temptation to despair is almost overwhelming when we stop to consider how the church is compromising with a cultural ethos that is becoming ever more flagrantly pagan. Yet by viewing the coming church struggle in the light of the biblical promises concerning God's providential care and the all-encompassing victory of his kingdom over the kingdoms of this world, we are able to see the hand of God in the present conflict and thus be reminded that God is indeed in control.

A second reason for embarking on this study is to share with my fellow believers the conviction that the real enemy is not the humanistic heritage of the Enlightenment (though this remains an adversary of Christian faith) but an aggressive paganism and nihilism that deny even the moral norms that the Enlightenment refused to jettison. The technological humanism of our day is the sorry culmination of the Enlightenment vision, but at the same time it contradicts the ideal of autonomy upheld by Enlightenment philosophers. It is not autonomy but conformity to the collective values of the nation-state that is championed by the new technological liberalism. It is not the separation of church and state, which has received support from traditional humanists, but the enthronement of the state or nation that presents the most dire threat to the integrity and independence of the church in our time.

In the face of naked paganism and idolatry, we need to

become far more clear about the mandate the Lord has given his church for our day. We have to become far more discriminating concerning the kinds of alliances the church enters into with social movements and more cognizant of the importance of sound doctrine in an age of latitudinarianism.

Whereas the commandment of the technological society is, "Thou shalt grow and change," Christians should emphasize the commandment of the New Society in Christ, "Thou shalt remain true to the faith once delivered to the saints." While technological humanism seeks to subject every area of life to rational control, Christians should sound the call to liberation from the fixations and delusions that the powers of this age impose upon people, preventing them from perceiving the reality of the human situation. Our task in this perilous time is to become free agents committed to the truth revealed by God and confirmed in the interiority of our being, rather than automatons who blindly follow the dictates of a technological elite.

This book is intended for an educated readership, but one that is much wider than the boundaries of theological scholarship. It is my hope that it will be seriously pondered by concerned Christian laypersons as well as by pastors and theological students. My further expectation is that this book will play some small role in equipping the saints for ministry to the world rather than encouraging them to withdraw from the fray into a safe haven of righteousness.

I
Introduction

If the foundations are destroyed, What can the righteous do?

PSALM 11:3 NKJV

"The days are coming," declares the Sovereign Lord, "when I will send a famine through the land—not a famine of food or a thirst for water, but a famine of hearing the words of the Lord."

AMOS 8:11 NIV

I must confess to a deepening conviction that both the mainline denominations and the conservative evangelical movement in America are more and more succumbing to the secularism of the technological society. Yet I also sense that the Spirit of God is at work precisely in the midst of the current social upheaval. Even with the collapse of moral and spiritual norms so glaringly apparent in modern society, there is hope for the renewal of the church in our time.

Unlike Jacques Ellul, to whom I am greatly indebted for his incisive analysis of modern secular culture, I do not see technological growth in almost exclusively negative terms.[1]Technology itself is not an evil—but it certainly poses a continuing and all-pervasive threat to the church because of its alluring temptations. I believe that technology can be harnessed in the service of the gospel, but I recognize that such a venture entails the risk of accommodating the Christian message to technological values. Utility, i.e., practical efficacy and tangible results, rather than fidelity to truth then becomes the criterion for evaluating the program of the church. The gospel is thereby reduced to a product for human consumption, and its capacity to judge human wisdom and achievement is muted.

This is an essay in social prophecy. I believe that we should seek not only to hear God's Word in the Bible but also to discern the hand of God in the times in which we live (cf. Matt. 16:3–4). We can see the Spirit of God at work in current social movements and crises, but we must never become subject to the delusion that these movements are bringing in the kingdom of God. At most, they can be regarded as signs and parables of the kingdom. Indeed, some of the revolutionary movements of our time may actually be signs of the activity of the powers of darkness.

I also hold that theology and sociology are inseparable. Theology without sociology is dead. Sociology without theology is blind. Theology is reduced to an explication of abstract truths unless it is related to the social crises and upheavals around us. Just as the Word became flesh and dwelt among us, so the gospel we preach must be incarnated in the situation today if it is to have the power to transform. Our task is not simply to *reflect* upon the Word or even upon the world in the light of the Word: our task as Christians is to *change* the world through the power of the Word.

We are living in a period in which we see the coalescence of the technological revolution and the erosion of the metaphysical foundations of Western culture. We are confronted not simply with a perplexing sociological problem but with a growing metaphysical vacuum. The crisis that engulfs modern society is more than social—it is also, and indeed fundamentally, spiritual.

The religion of the Enlightenment still holds sway over vast portions of Western culture, though this religion is now itself being challenged by a nihilistic Titanism, a pervasive attempt to bring down the established moral order. In America especially, both conservative and liberal ideology show the enduring marks of the Enlightenment.

The conservatives uphold laissez faire in economics, while the liberals defend laissez faire in personal morality. As Reinhold Niebuhr observed, the "faith of the Enlightenment is still the creed of the educators of our day and is shared more or less by philosophers, psychologists and social scientists."[2]

Enlightenment thinkers were devoted above all to the welfare of humanity, disdaining any serious concern for the glory of God. At best, they paid lip service to the ingenuity of the Eternal Clockmaker. The focus of their utilitarian ethic was the happiness of the greatest number of people. Our concern as Christians, by contrast, should be social righteousness—but social righteousness as determined by the mandate of the Word of God and not by ideological theory. Christians should strive for the common good, but they should not be subservient to the general will.[3]

The secularization of the modern church is painfully evident in the way it routinely follows secular fads. In the 1960s the emphasis was on social activism, especially civil rights. The rights of racial and ethnic minorities virtually became the gospel in many liberal churches of that period. In the 1970s the focus turned toward the interior life and interpersonal relations. The church bent over backwards to appreciate group dynamics and sensitivity training. In some churches, candidates for foreign and homeland missions had to undergo courses in group process before they were permitted to begin their work. The current fashions of the 1980s are feminism, peace, and liturgical innovation. The emphasis is on a worldly rather than an otherworldly spirituality. Many churches and seminaries, both liberal and conservative, are now making this new kind of spirituality their number one concern.

What is conspicuous in American church life in particular is the dissipation of doctrinal and apostolic substance. There is a preoccupation with the cultivation of the inner life and holistic salvation, but faithfulness to the apostolic faith, rediscovered and attested anew in the

Reformation, is dismally lacking. Voltaire's latitudinarian spirit has triumphed over the dogmatic stance of Calvin and Luther. Other views, we are told, should be respected because all views are fundamentally the same, though they differ superficially.

Mainline Protestantism, because of its departure from biblical moorings, has lost the capacity to be prophetic. Its social pronouncements no longer carry the same weight as those of the Roman Catholic Church or even some of the fundamentalist bodies. Denominations such as the United Methodist Church, the United Church of Christ, and the Disciples of Christ parrot the slogans of the peace movement and think that by so doing they are being prophetic. They forget that what the church says about peace or any other critical social issue should always stand in marked tension with what the world says.

The sword of the gospel cuts two ways and must never be used to undergird any social ideology, including pacifism. Vernard Eller, who takes an uncompromising stand against the horrendous evil of war, is nonetheless uncomfortable with those "peace zealots" who naively believe that they can bring in the kingdom by nonviolent protests and political strategies.[4] The key to peace in our time lies in conversion to the Prince of Peace. Not until human hearts and minds are changed can there be real peace among the nations. This by no means precludes Christians from working in the peace movement, but their particular message should be conspicuously different from that of their secular colleagues.

Lest I be misunderstood, let me hasten to say that I regard peace as the single most important issue of our time. Yet to adopt peacemaking as the priority for one two-year period and then to make youth the leading concern for the next two years (an action of the United Church of Christ General Synod in Pittsburgh, June 1983) is to treat peace in a cavalier fashion.[5] The same synod gave its stamp of approval to the Catholic Bishops' Pastoral Letter on War and Peace but preferred to ignore the stern warnings against abortion in this document. Like several other mainline Protestant denominations, the United Church of Christ has consistently taken the pro-choice position on this issue. The bishops wisely ask, "In a society where the innocent unborn are killed wantonly, how can we expect people to feel righteous revulsion at the act or threat of killing noncombatants in war?"[6]

What is disturbing and disappointing about the mainline churches is the selective nature of their indignation on controversial social issues. While vigorously upholding the sixth commandment, "You shall not kill" (except where this applies to abortion), they remain strangely silent on the seventh commandment, "You shall not commit adultery." The sexual norms and codes upheld by the church through the ages are dismissed as archaic, while the prohibition of murder is inconsistently seen as eternally binding. This accounts for both their intransigent opposition to capital punishment and their growing support for gay liberation.

The mainline denominations are, in my opinion, in captivity to the ideological left. This may be less opprobrious than captivity to the military-industrial complex, but it is still captivity and prevents the church from presenting a formidable and challenging prophetic witness.

The liberal churches especially need to draw upon the wisdom of Augustine who saw that piety, the fear of God, is the key to a just social order. Whereas Cicero had contended that order must be founded on justice, Augustine went further and held that justice must be rooted in piety, for otherwise the search for justice will end in tyranny. The church can make no more lasting contribution to the welfare of society than by preaching the gospel of regeneration and by devoting itself to prayer on behalf of those in responsible positions in society (cf. 1 Tim. 2:1–2). It also needs to proclaim the divine commandment, to call secular leaders to task for not implementing the gospel demands for social justice, but it must always speak as the church of God and not as a political lobby.

One of the greatest dangers today, which is discussed at length in this book, is the trend toward collectivism. The state is beginning to assume the role that the church once filled as spiritual judge and moral arbiter. There is an ominous drift toward totalitarianism in which the state demands allegiance in every area of life, including the spiritual and ethical. Thomas Hobbes' prophetic vision of the triumph of Leviathan, the "mortal god" of the secular state, is being realized in our time. The church is tolerated only when it is content to be a service agency for the common good (as determined by an elite of social planners who seek to enforce the general will).

With the growth of an all-powerful state with sufficient technology at its command to supervise even the private lives of its citizens, the church is being reduced more and more to a therapeutic operation that ministers to the psychic needs of people. Instability or nonconformity is seen as the dominant malady, and the role of the church is to make people fit for service in a technological society. Pope John Paul insightfully observed in a talk at Lourdes, France, in August 1983, "Today, the very sense of sin has partly disappeared because the sense of God is vanishing."

Since the First World War, it has been fashionable in some theological circles to portray the present age as "post-Christian," for it seems that the values of the Judeo-Christian heritage no longer dominate the centers of commerce, government, and education. Some commentators even refer to our age as "postreligious'—but secularism spawns its own forms of religion, and religiosity can thrive even in a secular technological milieu.

From a purely sociological point of view, the age we are living in may be described as "post-Christian," but from the perspective of eternity it may actually be "pre-Christian." No society or civilization in the past was thoroughly Christian, and the Bible predicts a latter-day outpouring of the Holy Spirit in the final days (Isa. 32:15–17; 52:10; Ezek. 39:29; Joel 2:28–31). It may be that the demise of Western civilization contains the seeds for the rebirth of vital Christianity. We may actually be witnessing in this tumultuous age of ours, in which Christians are more and more the object of persecution, the death and resurrection of the church. Wherever persecution of the saints of God abounds, the spirit of revival is also present. Wherever the devil seems triumphant against the forces of righteousness, the surprising work of the Holy Spirit is also in evidence, overturning the strategies of the powers of darkness and revealing them to be devoid of real power. Indeed, we are told that the power of the devil consists in his ability to deceive. He is the father of lies (John 8:44), and therefore we as Christians are obliged to listen not to him but instead to Jesus Christ, who has assured us that it is He who has overcome the world (John 16:33).

The age of denominations is coming to an end. Provincialism and insularism are being superseded by the need for a unified Christian witness against the principalities and powers of our time.[7] A one-world church, however, is not the answer to the problem of Christian disunity, since it in effect substitutes organizational strategy, even technological efficiency, for trust in the divine initiative and obedience to the divine imperative.

What we should strive for is a faith that is more conservative than conservative Protestantism, more catholic than Roman Catholicism, and more radical than liberal Protestantism and avant-garde Catholicism. By returning to the biblical roots of our faith we can recover the catholicity of vision that the church needs in our time as well as a renewed appreciation for the historical heritage that conserves and maintains this biblical perspective.

We may be entering the Age of Armageddon, but we may also be entering the Age of the Spirit when the new wine of the gospel will be poured into new wineskins. The evangelical renaissance, despite its tacit alliance with secular ideologies, is a sign of hope, and the same can be said for the charismatic renewal in our time. The crumbling of the moral and spiritual foundations of Western culture may be a divine opportunity offered to the church to rediscover its mission, to regain its momentum, and to become again the vital missionary force that it was intended to be at Pentecost.

II
Death and Resurrection

*
**

Today it is the myths of death, and they alone, that speak to us in our madness. The West is at its end—but that does not necessarily mean the end of the world.

JACQUES ELLUL

When the time of God comes—the time of the end and of the new beginnings—so it shall be that whatever in Christendom has become tainted and humanized shall suffer merciless collapse.

CHRISTOPH BLUMHARDT

We readily recognize that we live in a world that is becoming increasingly estranged from Christian values. In order to remain a Christian, one must take a resolute stand against many commonly accepted axioms of the world.

THE CHALLENGE OF PEACE *(Catholic Bishops' Pastoral Letter on War and Peace, May 1983).*

THE END OF AN ERA

We find ourselves today in a cultural situation in which historical Christianity appears to be in eclipse. This is true especially in the citadels of so-called Christian civilization—Europe and North America. This does not mean that religion itself is on the way out, but religiosity, even when it appears in the guise of Christianity, must not be confused with faith in a transcendent God who is Lord of all of life.

Our situation is not completely new. With the French Revolution came a widespread falling away from the historic faith. The radicals of the Revolution, such as Robespierre, wanted to outlaw all Christian worship; at the same time, they were amazingly tolerant of witchcraft, astrology, and other forms of the occult. Another possible parallel is the Balkan states under the rule of the Turks (sixteenth to early twentieth century) when the churches in that area had to learn to cope amid constant oppression. The last days of the Roman Empire also suggest parallels to the contemporary scene. Ancient civilization was crumbling, and the church was striving to maintain its identity in the face of rival religions that were seeking to fill the metaphysical vacuum.

What makes the situation today somewhat different is that the main enemy is the technological society rather than a specific ideology. It is our mode of life with its implicit values and assumptions rather than a particular explicit philosophy of life that seems to present the greatest peril to the faith. (I do not deny that various ideologies and mythologies are currently competing for the loyalties of people. Nor do I disallow the possibility that one of these new mythical visions will conquer, at least temporarily, and become the dominant or even the exclusive god in the technological pantheon.)

Part of the problem is that the Christian church has generally withdrawn from the public scene into a private enclave of righteousness focusing on worship and ritual rather than the crying needs of humanity, on personal piety rather than social justice. It is a sad but irrefutable fact that the Russian Orthodox Church at the time of the Bolshevik Revolution was engaged in a fruitless attempt to preserve its religious treasures (chalices, vestments, paintings, icons, etc.) and was therefore unable to relate meaningfully to the tremendous social upheavals then taking place.[1]

The spiritual movements of evangelical Pietism and Puritanism had a definite social thrust, and it has been said (for example, by the historian William Lecky) that the Wesleyan revivals in England saved that country from the kind of revolution that shook France in the eighteenth century.[2] Latter-day Pietism, however, has for the most part withdrawn from the social arena and has nurtured an individualistic piety that takes people away from the sufferings of humankind into an otherworldly hope. Karl Marx was not far off target when he described religion as "the opiate of the people."

The opposite danger is for Christians to identify with social movements of reform to such an extent that the spiritual dimensions of their mission are sacrificed. Christians on both the theological left and right have been tempted to align themselves uncritically with social protest movements and have suffered a crisis of identity as a result.

Liberal Christianity has been especially noted for its determined effort to establish the social relevance of the faith. It has been motivated partly by an apologetic concern and partly by a genuine compassion for the poor. At the same time, liberal Christians have not succeeded in breaking down the racial and class barriers in society. They have not been sufficiently anchored in the heritage of the faith to make a real impact on either the poor or on society at large. One of the foremost advocates of liberal theology today admits its failure in this regard: "Liberalism, with its ardent gospel of social Christianity, did not bring the Protestant churches nearer to the workers. It brought them nearer to professional emancipators of workers in the settlement houses and in the schools; there is a difference."[3]

The electronic church movement, with its conservative politics and theology, contains elements that inspire both hope and foreboding. While genuinely committed to the proclamation of the gospel, it is enigmatically ambivalent regarding the social imperatives of the law. It rightly calls for national repentance because of the sins of abortion and pornography, but it is strangely silent on the plight of minority races in this country, unrestrained military expenditures, the growing disparity between rich and poor, and the technological rape of the environment. Only rarely is there a criticism of military waste or a call for corporate executives to live up to their social responsibilities.[4] For the most part, the gospel the electronic church proclaims is not the whole gospel but a segment of the gospel. Nonetheless, this religious movement does minister to countless millions who are not being fed spiritually by the institutional churches, and its hold on certain truths of the gospel is not compromised to the extent that we see in the liberal or mainstream churches.

The area where religious conservatives can be faulted most is their glaring inability to discern the encroachment of the values of the technological society upon the domain of the church. Instead of warning against the pitfalls of unrestrained technology, conservatives generally welcome technology as an ally of the gospel. Technology becomes the means by which the gospel gains credibility and success in the world. It is legitimate to ask whether the gospel is not then translated into a program of self-help and faith into a method for gaining happiness and security— the goals of our secular, technological society. Communication skills take priority over the surprising work of the Holy Spirit in the dissemination of the truth of faith. Inner healing becomes a matter of the right technique in prayer, and the new birth is reduced to a series of steps that supposedly rest on empirical validation.

Too many political and religious conservatives as well as liberals have unwittingly accepted the rationalistic presuppositions of the technological society, namely, that human mastery over nature is a positive good and that educational technique is the key to the realization of this dream. Ivan Illich gives us this salutary warning: "Today, faith in education animates a new world religion. The religious nature of education is barely perceived because belief in it is ecumenical. The dream that education can transform men to fit into a world created by man through the magic of the technocrat has become universal, unquestioned."[5]

RADICAL FAITH

The need today is for a more radical faith, a faith that will return to its spiritual roots and that is demonstrated in this world through a gospel existence. Instead of accommodating the claims of the gospel to the highest values of our culture, we need to unmask those values as resting on an unstable metaphysical foundation. Instead of bringing the faith into alignment with social ideologies (e.g., classical liberalism, welfare liberalism, socialism, fascism), we need to expose the rationalistic and basically anti-Christian basis of these ideologies. Instead of heeding Bultmann's call to demythologize the Bible, we need to demythologize modern culture, exposing the secular myths that currently cast a spell over our society. Radical Christians will be iconoclasts intent on bringing down the secular towers of Babel, which often wear a religious label. Such Christians will be considered spiritual and even social revolutionaries, for they will be conspicuous in their refusal to pay obeisance to the false gods that enthrall a secularized culture.

It is well to bear in mind that the early Christians were accused by the Roman authorities of both atheism and anarchism, because they would not join in religious festivals and public spectacles. Their disinclination to serve in the military and their resolve to put loyalty to Christ over family loyalty, which contributed to the break-up of some families, further served to foster their reputation as a destabilizing force in society. (The fact that their sacramental rites were often held in secret brought upon them the additional charge of immorality.)

We are living in perilous times, yet also in times that should inspire hope and confidence. Secularism seems on the march everywhere, but we need to remember that Jesus Christ has already overcome the world (John. 16:33). He is already Lord—not only of the church but also of the still unredeemed world, though this fact is hidden from the eyes of unbelief. As Christians we can be assured that

Jesus Christ is preparing to bring down the dictatorships that hold people in terror and oppression. His church may be outwardly faltering, but this may well be a sign that our Lord is pruning his church so that it will emerge all the stronger (cf. Mal. 3:5). He himself is fighting for the poor (cf. Pss. 72:12–14; 103:6; 140:12; 147:6; Isa. 3:13–26; Hos. 12:7–9; Luke 4:18), and sometimes he uses the enemies of the church (such as Communists) to accomplish his purposes (cf. Jer. 25:9; Ezek. 28:6–7; Ps. 76:10).

We are invited to join him in his work of purification and reformation—but as his servants and ambassadors. We can prepare the way, we can announce his coming, but we cannot bring in the kingdom. We can set up signs and parables of the kingdom, but he alone can establish his kingdom here on earth.

Christoph Blumhardt (d. 1919), a German Pietist leader who was active for a time in the religious socialist movement, gives us this salutary admonition: "It is not *you* who conquers! The only Conqueror in the world is Jesus Christ. We must make way for him; in him we must live and move and have our being. We must stand up for him in repentance, crushed in our own being, sacrificing all that is our own, even the very best that we have."[6]

This is a time for celebration. The possible impending collapse of Western civilization will not mean the defeat of God's promises. It will not mean the end of the holy catholic church. It could even signify a period of new beginnings.

III
The Phenomenon
of Secularism

*
* *

I beseech you, my brothers, remain faithful to the earth *and do not believe those who speak to you of other-worldly hopes.*

FRIEDRICH NIETZSCHE

Contemporary incredulity no longer rests on science as at the end of the last century. Both science and faith are denied today. And this is no longer merely the skepticism of reason against miracles. It is a passionate unbelief.

ALBERT CAMUS

The motives, the processes, the mysteries that made man accept religion and expect God to accomplish what he was unable to do, lead him nowadays into politics and make him expect those things from the state.

JACQUES ELLUL

THE ADVANCE OF SECULARISM

What makes contemporary culture qualitatively different from medieval culture is the phenomenon of secularism. There was unbelief, heresy, and apostasy in medieval times, but the distinguishing feature of the modern scene is that faith in God has been for the most part relegated to the private sphere of life. Christian values no longer permeate society but instead are generally regarded as archaic or even injurious to the social order.

"Secularism" (derived from the Latin *saeculum*, meaning age or period) signifies a capitulation to the *Zeitgeist*, the "spirit of the age." It means not simply an openness to the values and goals of the world but the enthronement of these values and goals. Secularism represents a rival

religion, an absolutizing of what had previously been
regarded as penultimate concerns: the things that have to
do with the maintenance of life in this world.

Modern secularism has its roots in the Renaissance
and Enlightenment, in which the happiness and welfare of
man preempted the glory of God as the pivotal concern.
Belief in God generally continued during the eighteenth
century, though mainly as a means to guarantee virtue and
happiness for humanity. In the nineteenth century, the
God of biblical theism was increasingly called into question, and humanity itself became the object of veneration
and worship. In the twentieth century, humanity is threatened by inhumanity, and the very survival of civilization is
now at stake.

One may put it another way. In the eighteenth century,
the Age of Enlightenment, the devil was dismissed, at least
in the circles of academia. In the nineteenth century, God
passed from the scene (it was Nietzsche who heralded this
sociological fact). In the twentieth century, humanity is in
jeopardy, afflicted, it seems, with a sickness unto death,
indicating a crisis in meaning and not simply a crumbling
of moral foundations.

But something else is happening in our century. The
gods are being reborn. When God is dead, the way is open
for the return of the gods of pre-Christian times, the gods of
Volk, blood, sex, and soil. The Enlightenment desacralized
the heavens; now society and nature are becoming the new
domains of the sacred.

By giving ultimate power to the nation, race, or clan, or
to the scientific elite, secularism is preparing the way for a
new collectivism in which the individual is submerged
within the whole. This collectivism frequently takes the
form of a people's democracy in which the general will is
sovereign. Nietzsche astutely perceived the tragic outcome
of the death of God: "The masses will rule, the individual
has to lie in order to belong to the masses."

Secularism often takes the form of ideology, a theoretical justification for a sociopolitical program serving the interests of a particular class or party within society. Among the current ideologies striving to be king of the hill are socialism, classical liberalism (now called conservatism), welfare liberalism, fascism, feminism, gay liberationism, anarchism, and pacifism. Ideologies make social restructuring an ultimate concern and thereby become secular salvations.

It is especially disconcerting to see the church ally itself with some current ideology in the hope of gaining relevance or credibility. Ideological alignments accelerate rather than counter the secularization of the church. Christians are certainly free to work in any social movement of reform, but in order to maintain their Christian identity they must inwardly detach themselves from the motivations and ultimate goals of their ideological colleagues. And because their motivations and goals will be different, they will become suspect by the very people they are fighting for.

When secularism enters the church, the situation becomes critical, for it means the almost certain demise of traditional Christian values and concerns. Kierkegaard, who was even more vehement than Nietzsche in his denunciations of a domesticated Christianity, clearly perceived that the church was entering perilous times. His acerbic critique of the secularized church of Denmark has prophetic relevance: "Christianity in our times is close to becoming paganism; it has long ago yielded at least its main points."[1]

Reinhold Niebuhr was particularly acute in detecting the ideological and ipso facto secular character of modern religion. He contended that Protestantism as it developed became "a kind of spiritual sanctification of the peculiar interests and prejudices of the races and classes which dominate the industrial and commercial expansion of Western civilization."[2] He was especially harsh in his criticisms of liberal Protestantism, which, in a desire to

accommodate to secular evolutionary theory, overempha-
sized divine immanence and consequently ended in a
sentimental optimism.

Karl Barth, the eminent Swiss Reformed theologian,
was also alert to the intrusion of the values of the
Enlightenment into the Christian community. The result,
as he saw it, was a *Kulturchristentum*, a purely cultural
Christianity, in which anthropology replaced theology as
the overriding concern. In the liberal theologies of the
nineteenth and twentieth centuries, revelation no longer
gave information about God but simply yielded a new self-
understanding that enabled man to gain mastery over
nature. Barth poignantly perceived that the real object of
faith had become "not God in his revelation but the man
who believes in the divine."

THE GERMAN CHRISTIANS AND CURRENT PARALLELS

The German Christian movement in the later 1920s and
1930s signified the sorry culmination of culture-Protestan-
tism—an amalgamation with the values of the new paganism, in this case National Socialism. For the German
Christians, the goal of the church became the recovery of
German identity. The National Socialist seizure of power
in 1933 was regarded as "a gift and miracle of God."[3]

It is one of the ironies of history that that branch of the
church most infiltrated by the liberal ideology of the
Enlightenment was quickest to succumb to the beguile-
ments of National Socialism. The segment in the church
that ultimately resisted the ideological temptation of a
rapprochement with Nazism was the Confessing Church
which, under the leadership of Karl Barth, sharply attacked
the appeal to new revelations in nature and history and
confessed that Jesus Christ alone is the one Word of God.
While many pastors still imbued with the values of
conservative pietism or the old orthodoxy did not give

ready support to the Confessing Church movement, some having serious reservations,[4] liberal theologians found it virtually impossible to subscribe to the tenets of the Barmen Declaration, the creedal statement of the Confessing Church.[5]

Franklin Littell detects in our nation a mentality similar to that of the German Christians: "Liberal Protestantism in America . . . is very little different from the liberal Protestantism of Germany which accommodated so readily to nazism."[6] This startling accusation appears questionable until we stop to consider that the ideological temptations in our culture are somewhat different from the temptations in Nazi Germany in the 1930s. The dominant traditions in America are a democratic centrism (that hews to the democratic mainstream) and a social egalitarianism, and it is therefore in these that the greatest peril lies. Huey Long made the perspicacious comment that if fascism ever comes to America, it will come in the guise of democracy.

Parallels with the German Christian movement can be seen in those theologies and movements that seek a resymbolization of the faith and appeal to natural revelation. The focus in such movements is on the spiritual forces within culture and nature rather than on God's self-revelation in Jesus Christ as attested in Holy Scripture.

Process theology deserves special attention because of its widespread influence in the academic centers of theological learning in this country. Its goal is to replace the static categories of being, which have shaped classical theology, with the dynamic categories of becoming, derived for the most part from radical empiricist philosophy. Instead of the Almighty Lord or the infinite-personal Being of classical Christian faith, God is now reconceived as the élan vital, the principle of concretion, the Creative Process, the Divine Energy, the Creative Passage, the Directive of History, the Eros of the Universe, and the Principle of

Integration. Salvation becomes the fulfillment of human potential rather than deliverance from sin and death.

Appealing to the Renaissance and the Enlightenment, process thought portrays human history as the victory of persuasion over force (Whitehead).[7] Its emphasis is on the continuity rather than the discontinuity between faith and culture. Like "German Christianity," it is inclined to identify the highest values of the culture with the abiding verities of faith.

Bernard Meland, one of the more astute process thinkers, sees spiritual forces at work "in the sentiments and wills of enlightened people, seeking through education and experimentation, and ultimately through legislation, to carry America's culture into a new day of maturity and spiritual well-being."[8] He contends that Christianity, if it is to maintain its life, "will deepen its rooting in the cultural soil; but it will do so knowing that its spiritual fruition is universal in meaning and kind."[9] While deploring the racial overtones of the German faith movements, Meland holds that they "expressed a fundamentally sound discontent with the prevailing supernatural theologies which alienate religious men and women from their sustaining culture; and on the other hand, they revealed a commendable concern to turn religious devotion into a creative social force."[10]

Meland issues a call for the awakening of the spirit of a true nationalism rather than one that is insular, paranoiac, and aggressive. The time has come, he says, to celebrate authentic cultural heroes such as Thomas Jefferson, Abraham Lincoln, Walt Whitman, Ralph Waldo Emerson, and Henry David Thoreau. Taking issue with the anticultural stance of H. Richard Niebuhr and Wilhelm Pauck, reflected in their book *The Church Against the World*,[11] he vehemently insists that the church must affirm rather than negate the spiritual values and outreach of America's culture.

In a similar spirit, process-oriented Frederick Sontag

and John Roth call for a God that will be in conformity with the American cultural experience.[12] Thus they find the key to the renewal of American religion and culture in the affirmation of a "democratic God" who mirrors the pluralistic lifestyle of modern Americans and embodies the ideal of freedom. The cultural quest for freedom and the religious search for the new life in Christ are seen as identical:

> The search for a [new America] is very close to a religious quest, and it can become one if, in its course, we discover what God seems to be like now. The role of religion, in this American quest for release from an ugly or staid image, is an attempt to state religion's power to transform once again. The American quest for joy and release and loveliness of spirit is one with the religious desire to be born again.[13]

In their view, we are witnessing the birth of a new American religious mission comparable to but different from the original colonial quest for religious freedom. This mission will be to announce to the world a God "who is capable of relating to a postmodern, postindustrial future."[14] Americans are enjoined to embark on a spiritual odyssey that consists in sharing our unique values of tolerance, variety in religious experience, openness, and the spirit of adventure.

Teilhard de Chardin's process philosophy lends more support to modern totalitarian collectivism than to experimentation in democracy. Teilhard envisioned a cosmic evolutionary ascent that would result in an organic wholeness characterized by social cohesiveness—what he called "totalization" and "unification." He was able to appreciate both the fascist and communist revolutions as catalysts preparing the way for the coming world aeon, though he was not uncritical of these collective expressions of social ferment. "The modern totalitarian regimes," he said, "whatever their initial defects, are neither heresies

nor biological regressions: they are in line with the
essential trend of 'cosmic' movement."[15] In 1937 he welcomed Mussolini's counterrevolution in glowing terms:

> Fascism opens its arms to the future. In the solid
> organization it dreams of, more care is given than you
> find anywhere else to maintain and make good use of
> the elite. . . . Fascism quite possibly represents a suc-
> cessful blueprint for the world of tomorrow. It may even
> be a necessary phase during which men have to learn
> their business as men.[16]

It is also indisputable that Teilhard held to the
inferiority of certain peoples, which explains his advocacy
of some form of eugenics to deal with "unprogressive
ethnical groups."[17] Society would be required by the
mandates of progress and Christian charity to give priority
to those who demonstrate promise for the future rather
than to the rejects of life. He believed that the evolutionary
ascent would eventually result in a society based on love
rather than compulsion, and yet it was out of the excesses
of the new barbarians that such a society would emerge.[18]
        Perhaps more in contact with biblical realities than
process thought, but nonetheless seriously misguided, is
liberation theology, another example of ideological intrusion into the Christian faith. Liberation theology tends to
promote an accommodation with Marxist socialism. World
history is interpreted no longer in the light of God's self-
revelation in Jesus Christ but instead in the light of the
class struggle. It is believed that the kingdom of God will
be realized through the violence of a political-social
revolution.[19] Salvation becomes deliverance from economic
and political bondage. God is no longer seen as a supreme
intelligence directing history but as the power of the future
that gives meaning to history. Our hope is in the promise of
history rather than in the personal return of Jesus Christ.
        Those enamored with liberation theology would do
well to remember that the German Christians likewise

perceived religion as the catalyst that would cement the social revolution. They vigorously pressed for the convergence of politics and religion, both in theory and in practice. In the view of Emanuel Hirsch, the real theological need of the time was for the establishment of a political ethics.[20]

What is indeed perplexing is that many theologians who now warn against repeating the errors of the German Christians seem oblivious to the present peril of a synthesis with dialectical materialism. Liberation theology has made significant inroads in Latin American Christianity, both Roman Catholic and Protestant.[21]

An even more obvious parallel with the German Christian movement is to be found in feminist ideology and theology, which advocates a reconceptualization of the faith in the light of the new consciousness of living in a male-female world. God is redefined as "Immanent Mother," "the Womb of Being," "Eternal Spirit," "the Life-Force," and "the Primordial Matrix." Just as the German Christians sought to rewrite parts of the Bible and the liturgy in order to bring the faith into accord with the cultural revolution represented by National Socialism, so, too, a great many feminists are intent on rewriting the liturgical offices and biblical texts in order to bring the Bible into tune with modern democratic egalitarianism and a naturalistic immanentalism.[22] Just as the German Christians appealed to a reawakened national consciousness in their attempt to reinterpret the faith, so ideological feminists are inclined to base their case on the new cultural vision of a holistic humanity. Both are examples of how natural theology can undermine the distinctives of Christian faith.[23]

Like feminist ideologues within the churches today, the German Christians were seeking a more inclusive language for worship. Instead of acknowledging Jesus as Jewish, they portrayed him as cosmopolitan or sometimes as Aryan. Instead of referring to "the people of Israel," they preferred to speak of "the people of God." Salvation, they said, comes not from the Jews but from the eternal creative power within nature and history. Their emphasis was on the God immanent in the historical process rather than on the transcendent Creator God of the Bible.[24] Ernst Bergmann, who sought a new national church, even contended that the traditional belief in a "Man God" had to be replaced by the "Great Mother."[25] Professor Joachim Kurd Niedlich of Berlin, founder of the *Bund für deutsche Kirche* (Federation for the German Church), one of the various subgroups within the German Christian movement, was already arguing in 1926 that the hymn books and liturgies should be purged of all Jewish expressions and brought into accord with native German ideals.[26]

The new religious right in our country, associated with such groups as the Moral Majority and Religious Roundtable, more closely approximates that significant segment of the German church that threw its support behind the war policies of Kaiser Wilhelm in 1914. Protestant fundamentalists call not for a resymbolization of the faith, as did the more radical wing of the German Christian movement, but for a reawakened national consciousness that has its basis in Judeo-Christian values. They see America as the New Israel with a manifest destiny to be a light to the nations, a hope for the whole world. They do not seek a new conceptualization for the faith but rather a rapprochement between biblical faith and the American Way of Life. This, too, is a form of secularism. While it does not alter the root metaphors or original language of faith, it does tie the faith to a social ideology, in this case classical liberalism (now called political conservatism).[27]

Certain strands within Protestant fundamentalism could be susceptible to the allurements of a new national faith that might parallel the mystical vision of the German Christians. If this faith had a Christian veneer and appealed to America's democratic heritage, it would enlist the support of many earnest but misguided people in both conservative and liberal circles. Paradoxically, such a faith would be rooted not in the theocentric witness of the Reformation but in the anthropocentric spirituality of the Renaissance and Enlightenment.

A NEW GODLESSNESS

The Enlightenment sought to conserve the humanistic values of Western civilization without anchoring them in supernatural revelation. But a new form of godlessness is appearing which calls even these values into question. Dietrich Bonhoeffer put it well:

> The new unity which the French Revolution brought to Europe—and what we are experiencing today is the crisis of this unity—is therefore western godlessness. . . . It is not the theoretical denial of the existence of a God. It is itself a religion, a religion of hostility to God.[28]

A spirit of nihilism, not content with refurbishing the old order but seeking an entirely new order of existence, is pervasive. Albert Camus reflects this new spirit of daring freedom: "To kill God is to become god oneself: it is to realize on this earth the eternal life of which the Gospel speaks."[29]

The godless world of today is no longer satisfied merely to use the church for its own ends. Its goal is now to dismantle what is left of the church and to cultivate Dionysiac life (Nietzsche) in which the powerful affirmation of the self and the world supplants the New Testament call to self-denial for the sake of the weak and oppressed of the world. What is being threatened is not only the Judeo-Christian ethic but even the ethical values of the Hellenistic tradition rediscovered in the Renaissance and zealously promoted in the Enlightenment. The death of God means the demise of abiding moral verities as well.[30]

As Christians, we may affirm the death of God as a sociological fact indicating the collapse of faith in a theistic world ruler (as Nietzsche understood this). But we definitely do not subscribe to the death of God as the event whereby God empties himself into the world and lives as the spirit of the world (as in Hegel and Altizer).

From the perspective of biblical faith, God still lives, but he is withholding his grace from a disobedient people. He lives, but he is hidden in the cataclysmic events of world revolution and upheaval. He lives, but he is hardening the hearts of the emancipated men and women of our time to keep them from seeing the truth lest they be saved (cf. Isa. 6:10). God is present as Judge but not as Savior in a world that is constantly manufacturing new idols, even if these idols be intellectual constructs.

God is silent, but he will not remain silent (cf. Ps. 50:3). Even when things seem to be darkest, a light breaks through the darkness. Precisely when the world is bedeviled by a spirit of confusion, God is preparing to send forth his Spirit once again to renew and remold a broken society. The darkness of the modern age is a passage way to the new world aeon when the kingdom of God will be revealed in all its glory. The end of the world signals a new beginning. Humanity needs to sink in death and despair before it is ready for a new and perhaps the final outpouring of the Holy Spirit (cf. Hos. 6:1–3).

IV
The Darkening Horizon

The West has lost Christ, that is why it is dying; that is the only reason.

FEODOR DOSTOEVSKY

Culture necessarily degenerates where it is made God. Culture-idolatry is the sure road to cultural decay. If culture is to become and to remain truly human, it must have a culture-transcending center.

EMIL BRUNNER

The judgment upon Christianity is really judgment upon the betrayal of Christianity, upon its distortion and defilement, and the justice of this is that of judgment upon the fallen world and its sinful history.

NICHOLAS BERDYAEV[1]

THE CHURCH IN RETREAT

The past two decades have witnessed a marked change in the status of the institutional church in secular society. Benign and sometimes not-so-benign neutrality toward religion on the part of secular authorities is steadily giving way to open hostility. These remarks pertain mainly to the church in the West, though parallel phenomena can be discerned in the Third World and the Iron Curtain countries. Since the first World War, the church in Western Europe has generally been in a state of retreat, and this is also true in Eastern Europe, with a few notable exceptions, namely, in countries where religious loyalty and national aspirations coincide (as in Poland). But even where the church is outwardly flourishing, it is seen more and more as an adversary by the secular state.

In America, the church experienced a period of

unrivaled growth in the 1950s, but an erosion of membership and attendance set in in the sixties and continues to
the present day. Although conservative denominations on
the whole still show signs of vitality and some even
maintain a healthy rate of growth, it is appropriate to ask
whether their success is not at least partly due to the fact
that many of these groups shore up the traditional values
and goals of the culture. Churches that lend support to the
technological mainstream are generally rewarded by the
society at large. What this may indicate is not that the
secular society is becoming more receptive to the message
of the church but that it is taking advantage of the
opportunity to use the church for its own ends.

It is not just the statistical decline of the church that is
the subject of my investigation but the erosion of the
significance and power of the church in society today. The
church is confronted not simply by attrition but also by an
unmistakable antagonism to the values it has espoused
through the ages.

A secular, humanistic orientation is increasingly domi-
nating the centers of power in the modern technological
state, including the mass media, and this meta-ideology
regards both the Christian message and the Judeo-Christian ethic with open contempt.[2] The religious right is
perhaps more aware than mainstream Christianity of the
sinister threat of secular humanism, but it has not fully
grasped the fact that it, too, has largely succumbed to the
ideological temptation; in this case the source of infection
is political conservatism and nationalism, which prove to
be simply other varieties of humanism.

In the eighteenth century and continuing through the
nineteenth and into the early twentieth centuries, the
supernatural dimensions of the faith were under attack.
This can be seen not only in the area of biblical studies
with its destructive higher criticism and historicism, but
also in the area of theology, where a religion of immanence
usurped a religion of transcendence. The moral values that

are an integral part of the Judeo-Christian heritage nevertheless continued to command general support, but they were now rooted in conscience and natural law rather than in divine revelation.

THE ATTACK ON ETHICS

Today, the Christian ethic itself is under fire. Dostoevsky astutely saw that when God is dead, everything becomes permissible, and everything becomes a matter of indifference.[3] Jacques Ellul may exaggerate a little, but his grim observation has the ring of truth: In our time, "all ethical systems are either in ruins or empty."[4]

The Supreme Court ruling permitting abortion on demand (*Roe v. Wade,* 1973) reveals a nihilistic ethos in which the current fashion in morality takes precedence over moral law. The church through the ages has, with few exceptions, condemned abortion as well as infanticide as murder. Now there are philosophers and even theologians who are contending that the rights of an unborn child do not equal the rights of those who are making a tangible contribution to the well-being of society. The fetus is portrayed as a parasite in its mother's body rather than a human life to which the woman is privileged to give sanctuary for a time.[5] Some "enlightened" scholars even argue that the rights of a newly born infant do not equal those of a mature adult; these same people often advocate the killing of the hopelessly senile or those so physically impaired that they are left in a state of permanent coma.[6]

The extraordinary reluctance of the mainline Protestant denominations to speak out loudly and clearly against the permissive climate of abortion today is a sign of the widespread secularization of the church in our time. By favoring free choice over right to life, the churches have ignominiously succumbed to the liberal ideology of the Enlightenment which champions individual conscience over all external authority. The Roman Catholic and

Eastern Orthodox churches as well as some of the evangelical churches and sects have thus far resisted the pressures of the technological culture to conveniently dispose of those who might be a burden on the state; yet even in these communions theologians have voiced disagreement with the traditional Christian ban on abortion.

A similar pusillanimity characterizes the mainline churches' response to the rapid and unnerving increase of divorce with its resultant single-parent households. It seems that life-long marriage is fast becoming an anachronism in mainstream American culture as in Western Europe. The majority of marriages contracted in Sweden today are neither civil nor religious, so divorce is commonplace. A professor of theology at a Swedish school told me that whereas previously nearly every husband had his own mistress, now nearly every wife has her own lover.

Growing acceptance of a homosexual life-style also attests the erosion of the Christian ethic and the authority of the Bible. The fact that some churches (the Unitarian-Universalist Association and to a lesser degree the United Church of Christ and the Episcopal Church) now ordain practicing homosexuals, while others are giving this serious consideration, betrays a further concession to the technological amorality where the only norms are utility and productivity as opposed to fidelity to the divine commandment.

The breakdown of the family in modern secular society is only a symptom of the deterioration of the moral fabric that has held society together through the years. Radical feminism, which champions autonomy and self-fulfillment over mutual subordination, has in no small part contributed to the diminishing of family authority and responsibility.

The moral foundations of the faith are being subverted not only by the new left and the radical right but also by the democratic middle, which equates the voice of the people with the voice of God.[7] In the centrist tradition,

T. V. Smith and Eduard Lindeman contend that the democratic way of life recognizes no concrete truth except that tested publicly by science.[8] On the right, Ayn Rand upholds the ideal of rational selfishness as a justification for corporate expansion.[9] In her view, atheism is for the strong-minded and altruism for the weak-hearted. On the left, Daniel and Gabriel Cohn-Bendit urge the youth of Western nations to rid themselves "in practice, of the Judeo-Christian ethic, with its call for renunciation and sacrifice."[10]

There are further and even more sinister signs of the breakdown of cultural mores. In his play *The Screens*, Jean Genet advocates acts of evil as the only liberating force against the established order. This explosive figure on the French literary scene has been hailed by Sartre as a modern saint.

Genet's work reflects a revival today of the Marquis de Sade's pornography of power. The Marquis de Sade, who lived in the time of the French Revolution, sought to separate sex from love and unite it with cruelty and violence.[11] When the pursuit of pleasure ends in sadomasochism, we have indeed reached the nadir of civilization.

Even the ancient and almost universal taboo against incest is now under assault, especially in the Scandinavian countries. Yet such a catalogue of horrors is only to be expected. The logic of naturalism and relativism, so relentlessly fostered in our educational institutions, finally leads to the eradication of the bonds that hold family life together and keep the social order intact. The Judeo-Christian tradition is being challenged as never before by militant amoralists who aspire to create a society ruled by an elite of social scientists and technocrats dedicated to the pursuit of power and pleasure.

CHRISTIANS UNDER PERSECUTION

Today, the very freedom of the church is at stake. We are witnessing the actual persecution of Christians and not just an attack on Christian values. The gospel itself is under fire, and this means that the church is being challenged at its very foundations. Karl Barth saw the persecution of the Jews by Hitler as a foreshadowing of the church's persecution by the principalities and powers.

That there is a growing harassment of Christians behind the Iron Curtain no impartial observer would deny. For more than a decade, the Soviet Union has been experiencing a revival of Stalinism. Evangelistic and prayer meetings are labeled as "antisocial activities." In 1971 Yuri Titov, a Russian Christian painter, was committed to the Kashchento Soviet mental asylum simply because of his religious paintings. In 1979 a fifty-year-old Russian Orthodox nun was sentenced by a Soviet court to a hospital for the criminally insane. Her crime was making and selling belts embroidered with the words of the 90th Psalm: "Lord, Thou hast been our dwelling place."[12] Christian rock singer and composer Valeri Barinov was arrested in October 1983 for petitioning the government to permit the public performance of a Christian opera he had written. He was taken to a hospital where he was given repeated injections of chlorpromazine, a drug used in severe cases of mental illness. Some days later he was unexpectedly released, possibly because of the publicity this event received in Western news media.[13] A steady stream of similar acts of oppression in that country has been reported within the past several years.

Christians fare little better, and sometimes worse, in other Iron Curtain countries. In Eastern Germany, Christian students are denied access to the university if they try to answer attacks on Christianity in the classroom.[14] Romania continues to deal harshly with Baptists, Pentecostals, and Roman Catholics. Communist Albania has ordered a change in all citizens' names that are "unsuitable" from "a political, ideological, or moral viewpoint." To allow people to retain biblical or palpably Christian names, the authorities fear, is to run the risk of letting them rediscover their Christian heritage. Czechoslovakia is another country that has been increasingly inhospitable to the Christian faith.[15]

But it is not just behind the Iron Curtain that the shadow of persecution looms. Not long ago a seventy-two-year-old Swedish evangelist tourist was jailed for twenty days for handing out tracts on the island of Rhodes. Reports of the desecration of cemeteries and churches in Sweden and West Germany have been common this past decade. An official on ecclesiastical affairs in Sweden has boasted: "We are dismantling the Church bit by bit. And where necessary we are using economic means to do so."[16] The government of Denmark is presently refusing to renew the visas of evangelical missionaries from other countries, especially America.[17] In southern India, Bibles have been publicly burned and in one Tamil Nadu town the homes of some Christians have been set on fire.[18] Roman Catholic officials in Nicaragua, which is becoming an increasingly closed society, report that government mobs have beaten up on priests and attacked churches.[19] The persecution of Christians in South Africa is well-documented. Over one hundred clergymen have been victims of South African punitive action since the beginning of 1968. Restrictions on Christian activity have also been noted in Uganda, Chad, Zaire, Guinea, Mozambique and Ethiopia.[20]

In America the situation might outwardly appear more favorable to the church, but appearances can be misleading. I think a case could be made that ministers can no longer go out and expect the security and support of the community. Ministers who receive such support have generally compromised the stringent ethical demands of the gospel in order to accommodate to the goals and expectations of a culture that has steadily become more secular. Even conservative evangelicals, who traditionally

have held a Christ-against-culture stance, find that in order
to gain a hearing they need to demonstrate their allegiance
to the American Way of Life. Not long ago, I heard one of
the electronic evangelists make the absurd claim that the
way to gain prosperity and honor was to practice humility,
and I was reminded how far this kind of piety is from the
New Testament call to discipleship under the cross.[21]

Not only is there a disturbing accommodation of the
church to the secular ethos, there is also a growing hostility
on the part of secularists to the claims of the faith. When
Martin Luther King's mother was assassinated, the gunman
was quoted as saying he killed her "because she was a
Christian, and all Christians are my enemies." It was not
her stand for civil rights but simply her Christian identity
that made her a victim of the rage of a warped personali-
ty.[22]

THE SUBVERSION OF EDUCATION

This aversion to the faith extends beyond attacks on
individuals. It pervades the social structures of society and
is particularly prominent in educational circles.

There is no doubt that there has been a rising wall of
hostility toward Christianity in the public school system of
our nation. Franklin Littell goes so far as to contend that
the educational establishment, because of the power it
wields and its avowed humanistic orientation, poses "the
most serious challenge to Christian and libertarian values
in the entire society."[23] The values clarification courses in
high schools and colleges are designed to sever the ties
between children and the values of their families and
churches.[24] Value-free sex education proves upon deeper
examination to be in the service of hedonistic naturalism.
The phenomenological approach to the study of world
religions while outwardly scientific betrays a subtle accommodation to the latitudinarian spirit of the age.

Teachers in the departments of sociology, psychology,

and philosophy often admit their atheistic commitment and seek to bend their students in the same direction. Stanley Ballinger, an Indiana University Education professor, contends that "objectivity has no place in public-school teaching about religion, and that atheism has special rights and intellectual and moral superiority."[25] Writing in *The Humanist*, John Dunphy insists that "the battle for humankind's future must be waged and won in the public school classroom by teachers who correctly perceive their role as the proselytizers of a new faith: a religion of humanity that recognizes and respects the spark of . . . divinity in every human being."[26]

Arnold Beichman, visiting scholar at the Hoover Institution on War, Revolution and Peace at Stanford University, laments the growing ideological character of American higher education in which radical groups succeed in pressuring faculty to throw their support behind the revolutionary struggles of our age.[27] The pursuit of truth for its own sake is regarded as outmoded and reactionary. More and more, Beichman predicts, universities will fall under the control of government technocrats entrusted with the task of enforcing government regulations concerning faculty hiring, curriculum revision and admission standards.

There are other disquieting signs. Several years ago officials at the University of Nebraska forbade a Campus Crusade wrestling team to give public testimonies, though it granted freedom to groups promoting homosexuality and radical politics.[28] In March 1971, the Catholic University of America was compelled by a court order to allow the radical feminist Ms. Ti-Grace Atkinson to address its students and attack the Roman Catholic church as well as use obscene language.[29]

James Hitchcock has stated the situation well:

> Although America is officially religious, the actual thrust of American culture is really antireligious. Not

only is religion officially banned from public education,
thus inculcating the impression that it is false or
unimportant, but of all the options open to man probably
none is so lethal towards true religion as pragmatic
technocracy.[30]

The penetration of secularism into the bureaucracies
and academic institutions of the church is also something
to be deplored. In mainline Protestant seminaries, evangelical theology is summarily dismissed in the classroom.
Mark Branson, former head of the Theological Students
Fellowship, warns of a "Fundamentalism of the Left"—
the defensive reaction of the liberal establishment toward
the orthodox brand of Christianity.[31]

Catholic seminaries both in this country and in Europe
have been especially vulnerable to the inroads of secular
ideology. The reasons for this may be traced to the
surprising openness of the Second Vatican Council to the
world, an openness that was not, however, intended to be a
capitulation to cultural ideology and philosophy. The
unrest in Catholic seminaries and convents mirrors a crisis
of the utmost seriousness in the Catholic church. In avant-
garde Catholic circles, the confessional has largely been
supplanted by nondirective counseling. Priests are seen no
longer as spiritual authorities but as fellow travelers on a
road that leads nowhere in particular. One traditionalist
nun has described the state of those resisting the new
theology as "white martyrdom," because the persecution
they are called to endure is inward.

The later 1960s and early 1970s witnessed the politi-
calization of theology, and professors who resisted this
trend were often exposed to ridicule and harassment. In
1968 the theological group within the German Socialist
Student Organization directed this accusation against a
professor of practical theology at the University of Heidel-
berg:

He has advocated the imperialistic gesture of folding one's hands, which is, at the same time, an expression of submission and subjection. He proclaims the unconditional acceptance of the doctrine of justification and accepts without any objections the outdated creeds and hymns. But above all, he is willing to let mankind be subjected to a foreign authority (i.e., God).[32]

In the 1970s and continuing into the eighties, the focus in theological institutions has turned inward, and spirituality has become the dominant theme. Yet the turn toward spirituality has not been divorced from the social ferment. With social radicalism resurfacing, spirituality is increasingly seen as a catalyst for social change.[33]

Indeed, the new spirituality is decidedly this-wordly: we withdraw into ourselves in order to get in touch with the creative force within nature that transfigures the cultural horizon. Consciousness raising and social awareness supplant personal conversion as the chief priority. For the most part, the new spirituality is divorced from historic Christian themes and in many cases signifies a repristination of nature mysticism.[34] This is particularly true where process theology or radical feminist theology is ascendant.

Education, so it seems, even theological education, is more and more in the service not of the discovery of truth but of growth and change. It is not wisdom but technical knowledge that is deemed most important. It is not the opening to the transcendent but social restructuring that is given primary emphasis. This bodes ill for any society, since both social order and progress depend on a metaphysical undergirding.[35]

V
The Main Threats Today

Atheistic humanism both rests on and legitimizes unlimited growth of power, technology, and the economy. The higher the living standard and the greater the productivity, the more intelligent, artistic, cultivated, just, and good man will become.

JACQUES ELLUL

We live in an insane world. We have failed to perceive that man has become insane. . . . The world is again in the grip of polydemonism from which Christianity once rescued it.

NICHOLAS BERDYAEV

The worst error is to imagine that a Christian must try to be "sane" like everybody else, that we belong in our kind of society.

THOMAS MERTON

TECHNOLOGICAL HUMANISM

In his monumental work *The Technological Society* as well as in subsequent studies, Jacques Ellul has documented the thrust of the new secularism, which is aggressively hostile to the claims and values of the historic Christian faith.[1] What is becoming regnant in both Western and Marxist societies is a soulless technology in the service of pleasure and power. The criterion in the technological society is scientific rationality, with the appeal mainly to the social sciences. Behavior modification is taking the place of the conversion of souls, even in supposedly Christian circles. A culture that prides itself on demythologizing is succumbing to the wiles of a host of new demons, among which are race, the nation-state (*Volk*), the dialectic of history, class (the idolatry of the proletariat), sex, and science. Ellul has argued that the dominant god in the pantheon is *technique*, and I would concur that this is true for the present, especially where ideologies having their source in the Enlightenment are ascendant.[2] Even spirituality has become a matter of technique whereby we try to secure happiness and peace through methodical self-development. In conservative evangelical circles, it is common to hear of the various steps (or techniques) we need to take in order to be born again.

The norms of the technological society are utility, productivity, and efficiency. The goal is a conformist society in which every part is made to contribute to the growth and expansion of the whole. In such an ambiance, a person's worth is proportional to achievement. Those who can make no visible contribution to the general welfare such as the aged, the retarded and the incurably ill are considered expendable (as in Nazi Germany). Technological religion substitutes the ecstasy of accomplishment for the ecstasy of mystical union.

Every age, it seems, has a particular locus of the sacred. In the medieval period, it was the church. At the time of the Reformation, it was the gospel. In the Age of Enlightenment, it was humanity. In the technological society of our day, it is utility or perhaps creativity—the creativity of technical accomplishment.[3] Thus President Richard Nixon could hail the American landing on the moon as the most significant event in world history. This technological triumph was widely celebrated both as a monument to human ingenuity and creativity and as an evidence of humankind's increasing mastery and ascendancy over nature. For a great many Americans, it was also seen as a vindication of national honor. Indeed, other new sacreds such as nation, class and clan are pushing to the forefront and may become dominant in the future.

The heroes of the technological society are those who gain success by harnessing the latest products of the technological revolution (computers, robots, satellite television, etc.). James Bond is typical, and an examination of his exploits reveals the amoralism of the technological society.

Ellul has aptly called Teilhard de Chardin "the theologian of the technological society." Teilhard valued the dominion of man over man and nature and referred to it as the penetration point of evolution. In his view, everything must be sacrificed on the altar of "maximum efficiency."[4] Thus he could welcome the "new barbarians" (Mussolini, Hitler, Mao), for he saw no hope of progress without cultural purification, no matter how much pain and upheaval this might entail. He blithely regarded the nuclear testing at Bikini as announcing "the coming of the spirit of the earth."

Education in this kind of society is in the service of technology. Teachers become facilitators and therapists dedicated to removing obstacles to social change. What are valued are producers, not thinkers. The ability to perform is prized over contemplation. Serviceability and practicality are of more concern than truth. In religious circles, priority is given to that kind of prayer that has immediate verifiable results.

The technological society is invariably monolithic, since national and corporate growth demand the harmonious interplay of every working member. With some justification, Franklin Littell has described the main threat to the church today as a "monolithic statism." Paul Vitz observes that it matters not whether the society is rightist, centrist or leftist; by its demand for the total allegiance of its people, a conflict with the claims of faith is made inevitable.[5]

THE TREND TOWARD COLLECTIVISM

The alliance of technology and democracy results in technocracy, and this is what we have today in most industrialized nations. Here we see the breakdown of the old hierarchy and the ascendancy of the masses who are served as well as guided by the technocrats in control of the mass media and the vital organs of government. These technocrats prove to be a scientific elite respected for their dexterity in advancing the technological revolution.

According to Ellul, both socialism and capitalism serve the new technocracy. The "organization man,"[6] or more recently the "associative man,"[7] is given precedence over the rugged individualist or the entrepreneur of classical liberalism. A collectivist mentality prevails— the individual is expected to subordinate his or her unique talents and energies to the corporation, the union, the network or special interest group, or the nation. Robert Harvey speaks of a new tribalism in which individuality is sacrificed to the ideal of group cohesiveness.[8] In both Western and Marxist lands, a leveling process is insidiously at work, stifling personal initiative and independent thinking. What is valued in a technocracy is producers and consumers, not thinkers. The freedom the technological society allows is a consumer freedom but not a freedom to pursue the transcendent.

The expanding role of psychiatry and psychoanalysis in the trend toward collectivism is a matter of serious concern. The generally hostile attitude of these disciplines toward religion is underlined in this statement of Freud's: "The moment a man questions the meaning and value of life, he is sick, since objectively neither has any existence."[9] In Freudian mythology, we see the clinical reduction of the supernatural to the abnormal.

In the technological society, psychology and psychiatry easily become tools for bringing nonconformists into line with the general social consciousness or the dictates of the state.[10] In his provocative book *The Myth of Mental Illness*, Thomas Szasz makes a convincing case that psychiatry has become an agent of social control that identifies and immobilizes those with deviant ideas.[11] Soviet psychiatrists are now instructed to diagnose a "creeping schizo-phrenia" which includes fantasies of talking to God.[12]

The tragic flaw in the modern life- and world-view is sickness, the cure is private or group therapy, and the goal is social adjustment. Former vice president Hubert Humphrey echoed the new mood when he declared that to be against social security, civil rights, fluoridation and disarmament is evidence of "an emotional disorder," of an "acute detachment from reality."[13]

Such an attitude is more than fatuous. It is a sinister reminder of a creeping democratic totalitarianism that is already threatening individual liberties in the nations of the industrialized West.[14] In democratic totalitarianism the voice of the people is sovereign.[15] Differences can be tolerated and even encouraged so long as they promote common goals. What is emerging is a mass or popular democracy directed by an elitist group of welfare planners as opposed to a constitutional democracy with checks and balances. The aim of education in this new society is "natural development" and "social efficiency" (John Dewey). Harvard psychologist B. F. Skinner proposes that society be reshaped by behavior control technology so that people can be programed in advance to make those choices that contribute to the general welfare.[16]

As this trend accelerates, the lines between the people's democracies behind the Iron Curtain and Western industrialized democracy become very thin indeed. "Sociologically," Ellul observes, "there is admittedly a world of difference between dictatorship and democracy. But in both the moral problem is suppressed; the individual is simply an animal broken in to obey certain conditioned reflexes."[17]

Democracy as a social ideal contravenes all forms of racism and class privilege. When democracy becomes severed from its Christian roots and is made to serve expanding technology, however, new forms of racism and bigotry appear. In the "enlightened" democratic social

order, minority groups are discriminated against not because of color or ethnic background but because they
deviate from the psychological or cultural norm. Group
dynamics tends to make blacks more like whites, and poor
whites more like the upper middle class. The editor of
Commentary magazine warns that the whole idea of
"individual merit" has come under assault in liberal circles
and that if this principle is compromised, Jews will
invariably be harmed.[18] Anything foreign is distrusted in
the totalitarian democratic milieu, and this accounts for the
attack on foreign languages and support for classes on
human relations, education, computer science, and business administration. A reaction against the appalling
neglect of foreign languages in the educational curriculum
is now setting in, indubitably because America's increasing
involvement in international affairs is paralleled by a
decreasing supply of people equipped to handle them.

Despite its solid gains in the area of women's rights,
the modern feminist movement has in no small way
contributed to the technocratic, collectivist climate of
today. The feminist ideal is the coeducational school, but
this means that Catholic and other private schools could be
imperiled if coeducation is made compulsory. A trend
toward unisex in style of life and clothing, often correctly
perceived as an expression of rebellion, is nevertheless a
further sign of the development of a conformist, monolithic
society in the name of equality.

We should be careful, however, not to imply that all
those who favor an Equal Rights Amendment are motivated by a radical egalitarian ideology calculated to eradicate
sexual differences and roles. What I am trying to say is that
in supporting legislation designed to correct inequities in
our employment system where men are consistently paid
more than women for the same work performed and where
men are unfairly advanced to higher positions over women,
we should at the same time be sensitive to the rights of
minorities that uphold the patriarchal ethos. Such groups

also have a place in our kind of democracy where a certain pluralism needs to be maintained and pressures for cultural uniformity need to be resisted. The proposed Women's Equal Rights Amendment was condemned by four rabbinic organs already as early as April, 1972. One rabbi commented: "The central tenet of our faith is the uniqueness of the respective roles of men and women. . . . This amendment directly threatens our rights to continue practicing our faith as we have in the past three centuries in America."[19] The not illegitimate fear was expressed that suits would probably be brought to force mixed seating in Orthodox synagogues "even though this is a clear violation of our faith."

I believe that as Christians we should wholeheartedly support all legislation that equalizes pay for the same work regardless of sex or race. Sexism, treating women as inferiors, is a sin that should be unequivocally condemned by the church. But there is a legitimate as well as an illegitimate discrimination between the sexes, based not on the superiority of one sex over the other but on both biological and psychic differences.[20]

P. T. Forsyth was one social prophet who astutely perceived the threat of democratic humanitarianism to the faith of the church: "Between a Church and a democracy is this eternal gulf, that a democracy recognizes no authority but what arises from itself, and a Church none but what is imposed on it from without."[21] Democracy, he held, is the best form of government but as an all-embracing philosophy of life, it becomes a deadly rival of Christianity. If he had lived to witness the coalescence of democratic humanitarianism and technological humanism, he would have seen that democracy can present a threat to individual liberties as well.

In the more constricted society in which we now live, the way of resolving problems is by a refinement in technique. Ideological new rightists regard technological perfection in the area of weaponry as the key to national security. Ideological liberals see technology as the solution to teenage pregnancy and the rising rate of illegitimate births. For them the answer lies in new means of contraception and the universal distribution of contraceptives. Thus, what once was a largely a moral issue has now become merely a matter of technology. In this perspective, abortion is reduced to simply another form of contraception.

A democratic technological state governed by the principles of pragmatism and utilitarianism can easily verge toward a monolithic state that will tolerate no social deviation, a state in which religion is permitted only for the purpose of serving the goals of expanding technology and human welfare as this is determined by the technocratic elite. The withdrawal of tax-exempt status from Bob Jones University by the Supreme Court in June of 1983 is ominous, for it shows the state making its benefits contingent on adherence to the social policy of the nation. (This is not to deny that Bob Jones University is vulnerable to the charge of racism because of its stand against interracial dating.)

When the technological society takes the form of a corporate state in which big business becomes allied with big government and the emphasis is on persuasion rather than coercion and violence, we have the phenomenon of "friendly fascism."[22] Such a state may employ the rhetoric of democracy and even permit elections, but these should be seen as ratifying the consensus of opinion created in part by those in control of the mass media. It may well appeal to the religious traditions of its people, but its overriding concern is the consolidation of power and technological growth.

In Europe an aggressive secularism is much more evident than in America. In the Netherlands, Christian schools may now be required to employ homosexual teachers, i.e., those who uphold a homosexual way of life.[23] Behind this legislation is a radical egalitarian ideology with an obsession for affirmative action and antagonism toward hierarchy and other traditional values. The British Labor Party is increasingly falling under the sway of a secular ideology inimical to Christian faith, though the origins of this party are in Christian socialism and religious nonconformity. [24] In France, a flourishing new rightist movement is aggressively fomenting nationalist and racist sentiments; the Christian life- and world-view is dismissed as archaic.[25]

At first glance, the situation appears radically different in South Africa, since the churches there seem outwardly strong and Christian symbols abound in national life. Yet appearances can be deceptive, for beneath the Christian veneer is a society torn asunder by the heresy of apartheid—enforced segregation of the races. The "Christian nationalism" that gives ideological legitimacy to the ruling powers in effect testifies to the decline of Christian values and the triumph of the spirit of secularism. Some critics have maintained that apartheid has its roots in Calvinism, but this is a serious misreading of the situation. It can be shown that of the three Reformed churches the most liberal theologically is the most illiberal in racial attitudes, whereas the most consciously Calvinist is the most courageous in speaking out against racial injustice.[26] A confessing church is emerging in that unhappy country, inspired by the theocentric vision of original Calvinism, which contravenes all forms of cultural Christianity.[27]

THE RISE OF NIHILISM

Even more debilitating to the health of a culture than the humanism abetted by technological expansion is the emergence of nihilism, which heralds the disintegration of all objective norms and values.[28] Whereas secular humanism seeks to change existing institutions in order to bring them into the service of man's dream of mastery over the world, nihilism advocates the abolition of all cultural institutions and values in order to prepare the way for something completely new. It was preeminently Friedrich Nietzsche who laid the philosophical basis for nihilism by his strident attack on the Judeo-Christian ethic and his call for heroic self-affirmation in the face of chaos and nothingness.[29]

Nihilism is born out of disillusionment with the gains of technology and its penchant for collectivism. It is the last assertion of the solitary and strong-willed individual (the superman or *Übermensch*) against mass civilization.

The spirit of nihilism can be seen in the growing callousness in warfare reflected in the saturation bombing of Dresden toward the end of the Second World War, the testing of chemical weapons by the Soviet Union in Afghanistan, the destruction of Hiroshima and Nagasaki by atomic bombs and the disturbing but increasing dependence of nations today on genocidal weapons of mass extermination.[30] Any moral norms that may have been operative in war no longer have relevance in modern warfare in which there is no discrimination between combatants and noncombatants and where proportionality between ends and means no longer exists.[31] Nihilism calls for the abolition of the old order without regard to the moral codes that have held society intact through the centuries and for the creation of a new morality that sharply contravenes the "slave morality" engendered by Judaism and Christianity.

The disintegration of the family in our time can be largely attributed both to the secular humanistic ethos, which champions individual autonomy, and to a nihilistic amoral mentality that is openly hostile to the family. The slaughter of innocent unborn children by the technology of abortion mirrors a nihilistic attitude that pridefully spurns morality and decency in the interest of greater efficiency and productivity. Here we see the convergence of technological humanism and nihilism. What Ellul graphically calls the "violence against morality"[32] commands shockingly little attention from mainline Protestant churches.

The radical wing of the women's liberation movement,

by throwing its weight behind abortion on demand (what Mother Teresa calls "the silent holocaust") and calling women to create their own meaning in life without regard to any obligations to husbands and families, is preparing the way for a new slavery, which may well be worse than their servitude under an autocratic patriarchalism. Alexander Solzhenitsyn laments the plight of women under Communism, which in its Stalinist version is closer to nihilism than to Enlightenment humanism:

> We are always boasting about our equality for women and our kindergartens, but we hide the fact that all this is just a substitute for the family we have undermined. . . . How can one fail to feel shame and compassion at the sight of our women carrying heavy barrows of stones for paving the streets or for spreading on the tracks of our railway lines? When we contemplate such scenes, what more is there to say, what doubt can there possibly be? Who would hesitate to abandon the financing of South American revolutionaries in order to free our women from this bondage?[33]

Nihilism casts its ominous shadow over many other areas and activities. Surely the genocidal destruction of the Jewish people in the Nazi extermination camps is a glaring example of the triumph of nihilism over traditional moral restraints and values. The alarming increase in terrorist bombings, in which the victims are chosen at random and the sole purpose seems to be to inspire terror and confusion, is another powerful indication of the current upsurge of nihilism. This kind of terrorist attack is more characteristic of right-wing counterrevolutionaries than of left-wing insurgents. Likewise, the growing use and justification of torture (which technology is rapidly perfecting) as a means to gain desired information deemed essential to a nation's security portends the irrevocable collapse of the moral dike against chaos and anarchy. When technological expansion is no longer informed even by secular humanistic values but becomes an end in itself, we are verging toward a nihilistic culture that confronts us with a metaphysical vacuum of alarming proportions.[34]

The modern age, born in the exhilaration of throwing off the trammels of medieval thought, is by the twentieth century floundering under the pall of despair. In medieval culture *theonomy,* in which authority is centered in God, the eternal ground and goal of the self, was constantly threatened by *heteronomy,* submission to a purely external authority, in this case the institutional church. The Reformation succeeded for a time in recovering the vision of theonomy, but it had to cope with an emerging biblicism and creedalism. The Renaissance and Enlightenment, on the other hand, which celebrated humanity's emancipation from the grip of an authoritarian past, upheld the ideal of *autonomy,* the freedom to follow one's own light, to pursue primarily individual goals.[35] Now the appeal was to conscience and reason rather than to an infallible church or Bible. When modernity became increasingly severed from its spiritual roots, however, autonomy itself was imperiled. In the technological milieu of today, autonomy is steadily giving way to *anomie,* a sense of rootlessness and purposelessness.

Nihilism signifies the last attempt to affirm the self in an age afflicted by the anxiety of meaninglessness. It is a daring venture to live without the support of the moral codes and norms that have undergirded society in the past. It is a sometimes valiant effort to say yes to a future that is clouded with uncertainty. Nihilism is both creative and destructive, because it means fashioning a new world of meaning but at the price of evading our responsibilities to the people and institutions that have nurtured and sustained us.

On the horizon lurk new heteronomies, offering an almost irresistible temptation to people who struggle to cope in a society without direction or hope. The climate is ripe for people to sell their souls to the harbingers of a new authoritarianism in order to gain security from the enveloping chaos.

REBIRTH OF THE GODS

When God is dead, the gods are reborn. New deities are beginning to fill the void created by soulless technology in the service of secular humanism and nihilism. Jacques Ellul regards technique itself as one of these deities, but it can only be a provisional one, since the human heart needs a metaphysical absolute in order to give direction and meaning to life. The nuclear bomb is certainly another false deity, but by itself it is basically a technique of mass destruction rather than an ontological reality that demands submission in every area of life. The Nothingness of existentialism is the veil of a new deity rather than this deity itself.

Dethroning the God of the heavens can only result in the emergence of a new divinity having its source in the depths of the earth. Naomi Goldenberg calls for a return to nature mysticism, including witchcraft.[36] Reflecting a similar orientation, Wilhelm Reich and D. H. Lawrence find the new sacred in sex; discord in life is attributed to the process of repression.[37] What the votaries of pansexualism fail to recognize is that once sex is enthroned, it becomes demonic.

I believe that we are entering a post-Enlightenment period when a fascination with feeling and volition will supplant confidence in reason, when the depths of the unconscious will figure more prominently than logic and science.[38] The trust in technology will give way to a flight into irrationality. Technology will not be discarded but will be harnessed in the service of the will to power. Dreams and visions will be accorded new respect, though there will always be an attempt to explain them naturalistically.

The spirituality of the new age will have more kinship

with Gnosticism and the ancient mystery religions than with either deism or scientism, the credos of the Enlightenment. We might speak of this age as signalizing a new Romanticism, except that the destructive rather than the creative possibilities of humankind will be accentuated.[39] The dark side of the new age is already manifested in the current revival of Satanism and witchcraft, surely to be associated with the myths of death that will increasingly beguile the West.[40]

Marxism is a product of the Enlightenment rather than of Romanticism. It signifies the dethronement of the gods in the name of science rather than a return to pre-Christian gods (as in the German Faith movement, National Socialism, neomysticism and radical feminism). At the same time, nationalism is rampant in Marxist countries and accounts in part for the growing divisions among them. The conflict between Russia and China today is rooted in race and national rivalry more than in differences in the interpretation of dialectical materialism. The recent outbreaks of anti-Semitism in the Soviet Union are prompted not by Communist ideology but by growing ethnic insularism and nationalism.[41] The myth of the class struggle is slowly but surely giving way to a renaissance in nationhood and peoplehood.

It is my belief that the principal challenge to the church today is the rebirth of the gods of the earth, blood, and soil, a return to the ancient gods of the pre-Christian barbarian tribes.[42] War, too, is coming to be regarded as an epiphany of the sacred, as was the case with primitive tribal warfare.[43] Interestingly, Teilhard de Chardin viewed war as a catalyst in the evolutionary ascent and linked it to the glorious destiny of nations. Nietzsche, too, saw war in a positive light: "I welcome all signs that a more manly, a warlike age is about to begin, an age which, above all, will give honor to valor once again."[44]

National Socialism and kindred fascist movements called for the rebirth of the gods of tribalism, but the military defeat of the Axis powers postponed but did not preclude the emergence of a new religion of naturalistic mysticism, where immersion in the world supplants the ascent to God (as in classical mysticism).[45] When this-worldly mysticism with its accent on evolution is combined with nationalism and racism, we have the myth of the twentieth century.[46]

This brings us again to the startling and chilling fact that the dominant issue facing the church today is idolatry. When the living God of the Bible is dethroned, other gods, what Ellul calls "the new demons," will seek to take his place. The ancient gods of the Graeco-Roman pantheon are reappearing in new guises: Mars, the god of war; Gaia, the Earth Mother; Apollo, the god of light, symmetry and artistry (the perfection of technique?); Hermes, the god of commerce and theft (the spiritual father of capitalism?); Dionysus, the god of vitalistic intoxication; Pan, the god of the forests and pastures; Moira or Fate; Prometheus, the defiant Titan; Hermaphroditus, the personification of the mythical vision of androgyny; Venus, the goddess of love and beauty; Priapus, the god of sex and fertility; and Fortuna (Chance).

America's first strategic missile, developed in the late 1950s, was called Jupiter, the supreme god of the Romans, associated with lightning and thunder. Nuclear submarines have been given such names as Poseidon, the Greek god of the sea, and Trident, the three-pronged spear carried by Poseidon. I am convinced that these are signs that current militarism is a religious and not simply a political phenomenon.[47] Still another nuclear submarine has been christened "Corpus Christi" (Body of Christ), dramatically symbolizing the final blasphemy against the living God.[48]

The gods of nation, race, class, military valor, nature, technique, sex—these and many others are competing to fill a void that has been spawned by an antireligious secularism. Only Jesus Christ can fill the metaphysical vacuum in the human soul, but when Christ is absent pseudo-deities or demons step forward to claim supremacy.

VI
The Church in Disarray

<pre>
      *
    * *
</pre>

We need an evangelical revival as much deeper than that of a century ago as the Reformation was greater than it.

P. T. FORSYTH

Though the Church be desolated, the true Church of God lies invisibly in those who "have not bowed the knee to Baal," but simply and joyfully confess the name of the Lord.

KARL BARTH

THE DISSIPATION OF FAITH

The disturbing decline in church membership and attendance, particularly in Europe, is an indication of the uprooting of traditional religion by secular values and goals. Statistics show that no more than 6% of the population regularly attend church services in England; 4% in Australia; and 4% or less in West Germany, East Germany, and Scandinavia. In Madrid, Spain, regular attendance at mass has dropped to between 3 and 5% of the population. Whereas no more than 9% of Brazilians today are practicing Catholics, 33% are practicing Spiritists. According to one recent study, only 7.6% of Japanese youth have any religious faith. It is estimated that less than half of all Dutch Catholics continue to believe in the divinity of Christ, and fewer still accept life after death.[1] A 1976 poll indicated that only 29% of Britons affirm a personal God as compared with 38% in 1963. One in two Methodist churches in England now has fewer than 25 people at a typical Sunday morning service.[2] Over the past sixteen years the Church of Scotland has lost one-third of its entire membership, and this dismal trend is continuing: the church lost 20,000 members in 1982 alone.[3]

Although 90% of residents in France have a Catholic background, only 15% attend Mass regularly.[4] In another sampling, only 36% of those polled acknowledged Christ as God.[5] The Catholic weekly *Le Pèlerin* reports in a recent study that 90% of the French people no longer believe in sin while only 4% can accept this concept.[6] The precipitous decline in religious vocations is evident in the acute shortage of Catholic clergy in France; over one thousand Roman Catholic parishes are without pastors.

Since 1961, over a million Protestants and nearly as many Roman Catholics have left the church in West Germany. One survey indicated that if the churches in West Germany required belief in God as a condition for membership, one-third of the members would be compelled to leave. If they insisted on belief in the resurrection of Jesus Christ, two-thirds would have to leave.[7]

Those countries in Europe where religion has become an invaluable support in the struggle to maintain national and ethnic identity, as in Poland and Northern Ireland, are exceptions to this generally pessimistic analysis. Yet the question remains whether there is a rebirth of genuine commitment to Christian faith in these countries or whether religion is being used to advance nationalistic aspirations. The same can be said for the renewal of interest in conservative religion in America, where religious faith and commitment to the American Way of Life are inextricably intertwined. In all countries where religious faith is presently flourishing, overt resistance can be detected when the gospel is proclaimed in its full power and its ethical imperatives as well as the call to personal decision for Christ are sounded. One observer tells of the disruption of evangelistic meetings by Protestant youth gangs in Northern Ireland: "Noisy and ribald derision greeted mention of the name of Christ. But they were equally ready to lapse into their Orange songs. They proudly wore their

Protestant badges."[8] It is common knowledge that the dominant group within the Irish Republican Army is motivated not by Catholicism but by Marxism.

The growth rate in churches in the United States is stabilizing, but the downward slide of the mainline denominations still continues (albeit at a much slower pace than before). Roman Catholic membership is hardly keeping up with population growth,[9] though the evangelical denominations and many of the sects are still recording moderate increases in membership and attendance.

Recent studies of the American religious situation lend themselves to various interpretations. A Gallup poll taken in July 1983 indicates an upsurge of interest in religion among college young people.[10] Yet Gallup cautioned that only 12 percent of the U.S. population can be said to be "highly committed" to religious practice. Moreover, his poll showed that the perceived improvement in the spiritual climate seems to hinge on the enhanced feeling of personal "material well-being" among Americans. A disquieting study of Minnesota churchgoers in September 1983 portrays most Christians in that state "as theologically adrift on a tumultuous sea of moral and social ambiguity."[11]

American college youth on the whole continue to affirm the existence of God, though their conceptions of God are often hazy and equivocal. This stands in marked contrast to university students in France, forty percent of whom have no compunction in identifying themselves as atheists.

At the same time, the growing biblical illiteracy among young Americans reveals the gulf between religiosity and biblical piety. The trend toward a more permissive life style among our young people, especially in the area of sexuality, further attests the erosion of biblical norms and values.

Theoretical atheism, of course, is only one indication of the declining influence of the church in the modern industrialized world. There is also a practical atheism, reflected in the craving for material possessions, the rising incidence of divorce and venereal disease, and the accelerating number of abortions. In France today there are more abortions than live births; in Sweden half of all pregnancies end in abortion.[12] Even Catholic Italy has given legal sanction to abortion on demand. The U.S. Supreme Court ruling of June 1983, removing most state restrictions on abortions, is a sign that the abortion mentality has triumphed in this country.

The appalling rise in teenage suicides (5,000 annually in the U. S. alone) is further evidence of a metaphysical vacuum of major proportions in Western culture. The fact that this disturbing phenomenon is conspicuously present among teenagers from affluent families in our society shows that technological growth cannot provide a vision or goal sufficient to maintain the health of the social order.[13]

A NEW SACRALISM

The inroads of scientism and atheism are as manifest in America as in Western Europe. We are witnessing today the rise of a new sacralism, which invests with sanctity such ideas as the method of objectivity and technological programming. It is therefore possible to speak of "the magic of science" and "the mythology of technology." Michael Novak warns against the emerging scientific rationalism of the professional-scientific elites, those in control of universities, publishing, mass media, and the workaday worlds of finance, business, and politics.[14] Charles Fager goes so far as to declare, "We live in a nation that is not merely secular, in the sense of being emancipated from religious frames of reference, but is even actively pagan, that is to say contemptuous of and even hostile toward the values these traditions represent."[15]

But as we have seen, it is not only scientism that is flourishing today but also neomysticism and occultism. The age of technocracy is also the age of Aquarius with its emphasis on the journey inward. Yet even among the new mystics and occultists the spirit of technological rationalism is very pervasive. Religion and prayer become reduced to techniques that facilitate self-realization. A movement like Transcendental Meditation seeks scientific justification for its claims, and this is true of many of the other neomystical cults.

Christianity itself as a social-empirical reality is, especially in its American setting, in danger of falling under the spell of the cult of positive thinking, where efforts are focused on methodically cultivating a positive attitude toward life for the purpose of gaining peace and security. Even in evangelical circles people are speaking of a technology of the spirit, scientifically tested methods that guarantee happiness and inner peace. Spiritual progress charts and prayer chains play an important role in this enterprise. Faith healing becomes less an act of faith than a technique to bend the will of God.

When the age of technocracy, which paradoxically is also the age of Aquarius, becomes the age of Armageddon, mysticism will begin to shed its scientific trappings and become a servant of the will to power. There will be less appeal to empirical validation and more emphasis on self-authenticating experience. Self-fulfillment will be supplanted by self-deification or, what is more likely, group deification. Narcissism will be replaced by tribalism and positive thinking by a Titanic struggle for power.

Are there any signs of hope for the church today in this ghastly scenario? A balanced view will reveal that not only demonic forces but also the Spirit of God is at work in the church and world of our time. Secularism and nihilism pose unmistakable threats to the social order of the Western industrialized world, but they have also presented the church with new opportunities to rethink its mission and to revise its strategy. A part of the church is succumbing to the allurements of secularism, but another part is resisting their appeal and is confessing the historic faith anew, though quite properly in the language of our age.

PROMISE AND PERIL

The temptation in a book such as this is to focus only on the negative and to lose sight of those things that are more promising for spiritual renewal. While the church seems to be losing its hold on young people in Europe, Canada, and, to a much lesser degree, in the United States, revival is occurring in Indonesia, Korea, Africa, and Latin America. Even in an ostensibly secular nation like Japan, the Bible has become a best seller. The church now finds itself under siege in the Iron Curtain countries, but at the same time religious congregations—Orthodox, Protestant, and Catholic—are thriving even where persecution seems to be the most harsh (cf. Mic. 7: 8).[16]

In America we see a burgeoning of religiosity, but religiosity is not the same thing as biblical piety. What is occurring today is a growth of privatistic, experiential religion, for the most part devoid of doctrinal and biblical content. In the academic centers of organized religion in this country, the accent is now on spirituality—but a spirituality without theological moorings becomes enervating and destructive rather than creative. There can be no worship (doxa) done in spirit and truth without right dogma.

Mainline Protestantism as well as avant-garde Catholicism has sought to demonstrate the relevance of the gospel by identifying with social protest movements that purportedly have worthy goals such as peace, civil rights, gay liberation, and women's liberation. Both the World Council of Churches and the National Council of Churches have taken forthright stands on behalf of the oppressed of the world, but their indignation is selective, as Jacques Ellul has pointed out many times.[17] They are quick to raise their voices against colonialism and Western imperialism, but they generally remain silent concerning repression in socialist countries or Third World countries not allied with the West.

The church should by no means withdraw into a private enclave of piety and avoid grappling with the momentous social issues of the day. At the same time, it should speak a word from God and not parrot an ideological party line, which will most certainly empty it of its spiritual power. Forsyth's indictment of the Christianity of his day has signal relevance for our situation:

> Whole tracts of our religion are bare of spiritual passion, or spiritual depth. Christianity speaks the language of our humane civilization; it does not speak the language of Christ. The age, and much of the Church, believes in civilization and is interested in the Gospel, instead of believing in the Gospel and being interested in civilization.[18]

The steady expansion of bureaucracies in the churches represents a craving for power that amounts to a capitulation to worldliness. Church mergers are often encouraged for the sake of greater efficiency in organization and for the purpose of wielding greater political and economic power. We would do well to heed this warning of Christoph Blumhardt:

> If formerly the totality of mankind built the Tower of Babel, we now see *the Christian churches* building that tower. *They* want to be infallible, to be the greatest and most clever. *They* figure things out; and *they* will suppress God's word and, with their own words, bring in the kingdom.[19]

Luther sagaciously predicted that at the end of the age two churches would emerge—the Church of Jesus Christ and the Church of the Antichrist. It seems that these two churches will cross all denominational lines, though some denominations appear to approximate the true church more closely than others. Our Lord has declared that the wheat and the tares will grow together until the end of the age (Matt. 13:24–30), though false prophets will appear on the scene when Satan makes his final stand; those who have the eyes to see and the ears to hear will be able to distinguish the false from the true.

In light of the secularization of the mainline churches today, some scholars depict the community of the faithful as being increasingly on the defensive. Peter Berger has given this pessimistic prognosis: "By the 21st century, religious believers are likely to be found only in small sects, huddled together to resist a worldwide secular culture."[20] According to Martin Smith,

> Jews and Christians today belong to the dwindling minority of the religious people in the Western world. Majority and minority faiths no longer exist. The religions are a minority themselves, in constant danger of being buried by the Gentiles, i.e., the floodtides of communism and nationalism.[21]

While there is some truth in these dour appraisals, I believe that with the crumbling of the institutional churches and the shaking of the foundations of Western culture, a new church will emerge—purified of cultural accretions and equipped to do battle with the principalities and powers of our day.

One of the things that give me hope is the evangelical renaissance which, despite its ideological coloring, represents a powerful reaffirmation of the historic faith of the church. It is the evangelical wing of the church today that has taken an uncompromising stand against abortion on demand, the pornography traffic, legalized gambling, and the intrusion of secular humanism into the public schools. At the same time, it speaks with a divided voice on such issues as military defense, the conservation of ecological resources, the growing disparity between rich and poor, and the population explosion. Yet a growing number of evangelicals, and not just those on the ideological left, are beginning to address themselves to these social justice issues, even at the risk of breaking with their constituencies.

The striking resurgence of evangelicalism in America may augur a new day for both the church and culture, but it may also be an Indian summer before the total collapse of organized religion in this country. We need to be hopeful but at the same time cautious, for evangelicalism is not immune to the spell of the technological society. James Davison Hunter, a critic of evangelical accommodation to modern culture, points to areas where the secularist mentality has penetrated the evangelical enclave:

> *Sovereignty* has been translated to mean rational authority. *Providential direction of the church* has been redefined to mean the efficient administration of spiritual affairs in the world. *Divine anger, wrath,* and *vengeance,* if not eliminated entirely from Evangelical imagery, have been redefined to mean divine disappointment, regret and grudgingness.[22]

Another reason for hope is the bold prophetic stance of some Roman Catholic leaders, especially Pope John Paul II. Warning against ideological entanglements, the pope nonetheless calls for Christian solidarity with the oppressed and poor of the world. He admonishes both capitalism and socialism or exploiting and dehumanizing the working masses. He insists that the church remain true to its spiritual mission, but he also urges the faithful to live out the political implications of this mission. The forthright statements of both the pope and the American Catholic bishops on the perils of an uncontrolled nuclear armaments race should be heeded by all people who value fidelity to the divine commandment over national honor and security.

On the other side of the ledger, it is an undeniable fact that modern Catholic theology since Vatican Council II has manifested an alarming tendency to accommodate the faith to the spirit of the modern world.[23] Neo-Catholic theology, represented by Karl Rahner and Hans Küng, speaks of a universal grace at work among all peoples and religions; so long as we follow the highest that we know with the aid of grace, we are saved even if we do not possess conscious faith in Jesus Christ. In some circles of the new Catholicism, revelation is redefined as a new awareness of life and the world and faith as an open-ended search.[24] Many Catholic theologians are drawn to liberation theology, which seeks a rapprochement with Marxism. The history of the world is interpreted not in the light of biblical prophecy but in the light of the class struggle. Their expectation is that the kingdom of God will be ushered in through violent revolution.[25] Still other Catholic scholars are fascinated with process theology, especially that of Teilhard de Chardin, though Whitehead, too, is gaining in influence. They see the need for a new conceptualization that will make the faith credible to the scientific mind.

All these aberrations betray the compromise of the faith that inevitably arises when well-meaning but misguided theologians yield to the temptation to bring the faith into alliance with modernity. What the church needs today is people of an entirely different stripe, people who will stand firm for the faith even at the risk of losing life, possessions, and respectability.

VII
New Models
for the Church

*
**

Only where graves are is the resurrection.

FRIEDRICH NIETZSCHE

There is need today for a theology of courage—of holy daring, saintly boldness—which may serve to justify the way of human beings with what has immemorially been called God.

ROGER HAZELTON

A saint has to be a misfit. A person who embodies what his culture considers typical or normal cannot be exemplary.

MARTIN MARTY

A NEW KIND OF SAINT

The church in every age needs models, people in whom the passion and victory of Jesus Christ are palpably manifest. As Christians, we are all called to be saints, but there are some who have been specially chosen by God to make a public witness that patently reveals the judgment of God upon human sin. We are all called to radiate the light of Christ, but only some are given the privilege of bearing this light in the face of open and flagrant opposition. We are all expected to take up the cross and follow Christ, but only some carry a cross that poses a direct challenge to the principalities and powers of the world. Only some therefore can be considered *saints* in the special sense of being public signs of the passion and victory of Jesus Christ.

This is not to denigrate the unsung and unknown saints who have had to break with friends or family or who have lost jobs or the hope of promotion for taking a stand for what they know to be right. Or the mother who has been left on her own to care for five children and who survives on next-to-nothing and a living faith in God. But it is to insist that those singled out for public rebuke and opprobrium, especially those who die for the faith, should be given signal recognition and honor by the church, since the sufferings of these people become dramatically visible to the world at large. These saints are not necessarily more worthy, but in the providence of God their story succeeds in capturing the imagination of untold numbers, both believers and unbelievers, and can therefore be used by the church to instruct its children on the meaning of discipleship and to proclaim anew to the world the cross and resurrection victory of Jesus Christ. To be sure, any real sacrifice for the faith that comes to public attention and poignantly demonstrates the cost of discipleship lends itself to commemoration by the church. The Epistle to the Hebrews does not hesitate to rejoice in the heroism of particular Old Testament saints (ch. 11).

Every period in the church has had its celebrated representatives of the sacred. In the early church, martyrs and anchorites were held in high esteem. The medieval church accorded similar honor to monks and nuns, both contemplative and active. The Reformation period eulogized those who were concerned for purity in doctrine and liturgy, who pioneered in church reform. Biblical preachers and missionaries were the models for the Pietists and Puritans. In the 1960s and early 1970s, social activists, those who made a public protest against social wrongs, were held to be exemplary of true Christian faith. Some of the leading figures involved in the social upheavals of that period were Camilo Torres; Clarence Jordan, founder of the interracial Koinonia Farm; James Reeb, who gave his life at Selma; Martin Luther King; Dorothy Day; and Philip and Daniel Berrigan.

I suggest that the models of the future will again be the martyrs and confessors of the faith,* those who are persecuted primarily because of their Christian identity. These are people who will suffer for the sake of the gospel itself and not simply for the cause of social righteousness. These are the people who will boldly confess that Jesus Christ alone is Savior and Lord; that we are justified only by free grace and not by works, even humanitarian works; and that Holy Scripture and not reason or even religious experience is the infallible authority for faith and practice. They will bear uncompromising witness to the infinite-personal God of biblical faith, the ontological Trinity of Father, Son, and Holy Spirit, in the face of the false gods of race, class, nation, sex, and technological programming.

The demonstration of a Christian life will still be important, but it is the proclamation of the gospel that will arouse the special ire of a secularized world. Life and words, of course, go together, but the stumbling block that will elicit the rage of the world is Jesus Christ himself and those who bear witness to him (cf. John 15:18–20; Acts 4:24–26).

What I am suggesting is that the Christian message itself will become the object of ridicule. The life of discipleship will be derided precisely because it calls attention to the gospel, to its claims and imperatives. We are entering an age in which the simple confession of faith becomes the dividing line between the reprobate and the elect, the oppressors and the oppressed, the children of darkness and the children of light.

TWENTIETH-CENTURY SAINTS

In perhaps no other century has the church seen so many confessors and martyrs to the faith as in this one. Countless

---

*Confessors are those who confess the faith under persecution but do not actually suffer death for their convictions. Church historians have traditionally referred to these people as "white martyrs."

Christians have placed their lives on the line for the gospel. Most of these witnesses to the passion and victory of Christ are relatively unknown, but some have become public signs of God's kingdom. I have in mind a number of candidates for sainthood in the new religious situation in which we find ourselves—people who have refused to bow the knee to Baal and whose stories have increasing significance for our time.

One powerful sign of the kingdom in our time is Paul Schneider, a German Reformed clergyman, who became known as the pastor of Buchenwald prison.[1] He was arrested because he fearlessly proclaimed from his pulpit that Jesus alone is Lord, and this immediately challenged the pretensions of Hitler, who claimed to be the only Savior and Führer of Germany. When Schneider was told by the Gestapo to cease preaching the exclusivistic claims of the gospel because his children might become orphans, he replied, "Better that they should be orphans than grow up and know that their father bowed down to the devil instead of to the living God."

Incarcerated in the notorious Buchenwald prison, Schneider was soon placed in solitary confinement because he would not keep quiet concerning the uncompromising demands and infallible promises of the gospel. He eventually died of the ill effects of torture, but even from his solitary cell his voice could often be heard consoling his fellow prisoners in the faith and castigating his guards, calling them to repentance.

In the same period, Dietrich Bonhoeffer, a then relatively unknown German Lutheran pastor and theologian, aroused the ire of the Nazis by his radio address attacking the Nazi leadership principle and also by his open support of the Confessing Church movement.[2] Having founded what soon became an underground seminary at Finkenwalde in Pomerania, he demonstrated in his own life what he had urged on others—that fidelity to the kingdom of God takes precedence over all other loyalties, including that which we owe to our nation. By the late 1930s, Bonhoeffer's activities were greatly restricted by the Gestapo. Two of his former professors at Union Theological Seminary in New York succeeded in bringing him safely to America, but he could not allow himself to remain in this refuge, detached from the sufferings of his people. Against his teachers' advice, he boldly decided to return to Germany, even though by this time he was a marked man.

After the war began, Bonhoeffer, despite his pacifist convictions, was led to participate in a resistance group that eventually plotted to assassinate Hitler. In April 1943 he was arrested by the Gestapo and imprisoned at Tegel in Berlin. While in prison, he had an opportunity to escape, but he called off the escape plans for fear of reprisals against his family. Although often tempted to despair, he radiated a joy and peace that were a constant source of inspiration to his fellow prisoners. He was hanged on the gallows in the Flossenbürg prison camp in April 1945.

It is interesting to compare Dietrich Bonhoeffer and Paul Schneider, both of whom were exceptional Christians. Bonhoeffer was arrested because of his illegal activities in the resistance movement. Schneider was taken into custody simply because of his confession that Jesus alone is Lord. Bonhoeffer has been hailed by secular and political theologians as an outstanding example of political involvement on behalf of the oppressed. What they have not sufficiently discerned is that Bonhoeffer's political acts were motivated by a deep religious faith in the God of the Bible, by an unequivocal commitment to the gospel of reconciliation and redemption. Bonhoeffer will come to be appreciated in this new age of persecution for his devotion to Jesus Christ and not simply for his political heroism.

The same passionate commitment to our Savior characterized Corrie and Betsy ten Boom, whose sacrificial lives became the subject of the film *The Hiding Place*. Imprisoned in the infamous Ravensbrück concentration camp for hiding Jews from the Nazis, these two Dutch sisters were a source of spiritual consolation to their fellow inmates.[3] Betsy died in prison from beatings and malnutrition, but Corrie was released due to a clerical error. In her remaining years, she traveled around the world giving testimony to the power of God to save and comfort the afflicted.

The Ten Booms have received favorable attention in the secular media because of their involvement in the resistance movement on behalf of the Jews. But what is not commonly known is that their first commitment was to evangelism. It was their evangelistic zeal in conducting illegal prayer meetings in Ravensbrück that brought upon them the wrath of the German guards. It was their fidelity to Jesus Christ, the Messiah of Israel, that prompted them to defy the Nazi interdict against the Jews, who still remained in some sense God's special people. Christians today should look to these two sisters for inspiration because of both their social involvement on behalf of the oppressed and their steadfast commitment to the faith once delivered to the saints.

Nor should we forget the challenging witness of Franz Jägerstätter, an Austrian Catholic layman who was beheaded by the Nazis in August 1943.[4] Although not directly involved in political subversion, he did make a public confession of faith in Christ in open defiance of the Nazi regime, refusing to serve in the German army. It was not simply his refusal to be a soldier but his reason for refusing, namely, his intransigent opposition to Nazism, that led to his arrest, imprisonment, and execution. He recognized that loyalty to Christ and the gospel conflicted with loyalty to the Führer and Nazism. He was well aware of the fact that one had to take the oath of unconditional allegiance to the Führer upon induction in Hitler's army . He also saw that Hitler was waging a war that involved the shameful slaughter of innocent people. To serve in the military would therefore be tantamount to apostasy.

Jägerstätter was motivated not by pacifist convictions,[5] nor by romantic idealism, but simply by fidelity to the gospel. He could have been saved had he agreed to noncombatant service. After his arrest and incarceration he was given the opportunity to regain his freedom. But he adamantly refused to cooperate with a regime that was persecuting the church and demanding the kind of loyalty that should be reserved only for God.

Even closer to our own day is Richard Wurmbrand, a Rumanian Lutheran pastor who was imprisoned by the Communists for more than fourteen years.[6] His crime was his stubborn persistence in witnessing to Jesus Christ publicly. Subjected to relentless interrogation, beatings, torture, and attempted brainwashing, he adamantly refused to renounce his faith. Instead, he sought to win his tormentors to Jesus Christ, in some cases succeeding. When in solitary confinement, he would tap out the gospel story by Morse code, which resulted in the conversions of a number of his fellow prisoners.

After his release in June 1964, Wurmbrand worked with the underground church in Rumania until Christian organizations in the West paid a ransom of approximately $10,000 to the Rumanian government, making it possible for him and his family to begin a new life and ministry outside the Communist orbit. Richard Wurmbrand has been an embarrassment to the World Council of Churches because of its policy of not giving unnecessary offense to the Communist countries, but the authenticity of his life and witness cannot be doubted.

Equally engrossing is the story of Boris M. Zdorovets, one of the best-known Baptist preachers in Russia.[7] His offense was leading an unauthorized open-air service attended by two thousand people on May 2, 1973. In 1972 he had completed a ten-year sentence for unauthorized religious activities. Because of his persistence in public witnessing, he was sentenced to three years in solitary confinement in a "severe" labor camp and seven years in exile. His only crime was his passion to tell the story of salvation to the spiritually lost.

Signal recognition should also be given to Father Sthjefen Kurti, a seventy-year-old Roman Catholic priest, who was executed by an Albanian firing squad in April 1973.[8] He had spent eighteen years in a Communist prison for "spying for the Vatican." He was sentenced again in 1967 to an additional sixteen years for opposing government efforts to destroy his parish church. While in detention, he exercised his priesthood secretly and baptized the child of a woman prisoner. For this he was put on trial by Albanian authorities and later handed over to a military firing squad. The rite of Christian baptism was regarded by secular authorities as a seditious act; such is the fanatical intolerance of modern militant atheism.

Still another redoubtable warrior of the faith who proved his mettle in battle with the principalities and powers was Cardinal Mindszenty of Hungary.[9] Because of his association with politically conservative movements in his country, it has become fashionable in avant-garde Catholic circles to ignore or excuse his sufferings at the hands of the Communist Party in postwar Hungary. He was arrested in December 1948 on mainly trumped-up charges of treason, conspiracy, and the misuse of foreign currency. After a month of torture and interrogation, followed by an orchestrated show trial, he was convicted and sentenced to life imprisonment. He then took refuge in the American embassy in Budapest. The Vatican was able to secure his release only much later, and he spent his last years in exile in Rome.

Cardinal Mindszenty has placed the post-Vatican II Catholic Church in an awkward position because of his tie to the old established order and his militant anti-Communism. Yet his fidelity to his faith proved to be unflinching even under harassment and torture. He was subjected to insults and ignominy mainly because of his identification with the Catholic church and because he placed loyalty to his Savior above loyalty to the state. This fact will be more and more appreciated as the church throughout the world becomes the object of persecution.

Many other noted martyrs and confessors of the faith in our time could be mentioned: Nate Saint, a missionary pilot with the Missionary Aviation Fellowship, who was killed by the Auca Indians in Ecuador together with three fellow missionaries;[10] Evelyn Anderson and Beatrice Kosin, representing Christian Missions in Many Lands, who were tied to a post and burned alive in a grass hut in southern Laos by the Viet Cong toward the end of the Vietnamese war; Paul Carlson, Covenant missionary who was shot down by black nationalists in the Congo in the early 1960s;[11] Georgi Vins, Baptist pastor imprisoned in Russia in 1974 for preaching the gospel;[12] Alexander Solzhenitsyn, who suffered for many years in Russian prisons and detention camps because of his outspoken denunciation of Communist totalitarianism, informed by a deepening devotion to Christ;[13] Desmond Tutu, black Anglican bishop, who lives under constant harassment and surveillance in South Africa because of his courageous witness to the promises and demands of the gospel;[14] and Watchman Nee, a member of the Little Flock, who was tortured by the Communist government in China and died in prison in June 1972. What distinguishes all these men and women is that they have pledged ultimate allegiance to Jesus Christ and not to the state, party, or scientific elite. Their deeds deserve to be commemorated by the church at large because they can be regarded as modern martyrs and confessors of the age-old faith (cf. Heb. 11).

I predict that the call to sainthood will soon be rediscovered by a church that has been undermined by accommodation to worldly values and that consequently elevates secular heroes over Christian saints. It is a call that extends to all believers, but only some are granted the privilege of red or white martyrdom, and it is these who should be given special recognition by a church sorely in need of models to challenge its people, especially its youth.

Yet is not just for individual Christians to make a courageous, forthright witness but also for institutions— churches and seminaries. With the emergence of a militant secularism and the recrudescence of paganism, the church, in order to remain true to its vocation, must be a church under the cross.

VIII
The Challenge Facing Churches and Seminaries

The people wander like sheep; they are afflicted for want of a shepherd.

ZECHARIAH 10:2 (RSV)

A warm spirituality without the apostolic and evangelical substance may seem attractive to many—what is called undogmatic, or even unconscious Christianity. It will specially appeal to the lay mind, in the pulpit and out. But it is death to a Church.

P. T. FORSYTH

No less is at stake here than the unity of the Church among other things. The cleavage in the understanding of the Gospel can be so deep as to drive us to Luther's words about "two churches," the Church of God and the church of anti-Christ.

HELMUT GOLLWITZER

AN EMERGING CONFESSIONAL SITUATION

In the face of mounting secularization, the church must take a stand for both the purity of the faith and the crying needs of humanity. It must address itself to the threat of heresy from within as well as to pressing social evils. The sword of the gospel must first cut into the church before it can cut into the world.

The surest way to reaffirm orthodoxy is to rediscover heresy. The erosion of the faith of the church begins from within, and usually by the time it is widely perceived, considerable damage has been done. A church that does not take theology seriously is unwittingly encouraging understandings of the faith that are warped or unbalanced. A church can ignore laxity or reluctance in affirming the

dogmas of the faith only at its peril. Its primary concern in
this area is not to root out heretics but to protect the
faithful. The church is to be a guardian of souls as well as a
power house of evangelism (cf. Ezek. 33, 34).

The outward acceptance of the church by secular
culture can be deceptive, especially in our American
situation. A church that simply gives divine sanction to the
cultural status quo or tacit if not explicit approval to the
values of the surrounding culture has compromised its
integrity. A church that prospers in a pagan environment is
not necessarily one that has remained true to its Lord.

In a time when the fundamentals of the faith are being
called into question, when the gospel itself is being
reinterpreted in the light of current world views, we have
to ask ourselves whether we are not in fact entering a
confessional situation (*status confessionis*). In such a
situation, the church needs to redefine itself in order to
maintain its integrity and identity. It needs to confess anew
the age-old faith in the language of its day, and this will
entail warning against deviations that signify an accommodation to cultural values and ideologies.

A confessing church will speak to the burning issues of
the time, both theological and ethical. How can the church
give a faithful witness to its Lord and Savior and remain
silent in the face of abortion on demand, the breakdown of
the family, the idolatry of weapons of mass extermination,
and the growing disparity between rich and poor? How can
a church based on the gospel close its eyes to growing
syncretism and eclecticism in which Jesus is depicted as
only a great prophet, a spiritual guru, but not as the divine
Savior and Lord of the world?

A genuine confession of faith will be addressed to the
whole church, not simply to a part of the church. It will be
regarded by those who embrace it as God's self-witness to
his revelation in their own place and time. As the standard
of a confessing church, it will always be under Holy
Scripture and therefore open to future revision and correc-

tion. It will be seen not as a new law but instead as a concrete declaration expressing the divine imperative for our situation. Karl Barth has aptly declared, "'Confessions' exist for us to go through them (not once but continually), not for us to return to them" and "take up our abode in them."[1] Confessions are broken symbols that nonetheless convey the infallible divine promise and the absolutely binding divine commandment to a church that has strayed from the age-old paths (cf. Jer. 6:16; 18:15).

Like their parent denominations, theological seminaries today need to get beyond a narrow parochialism and adopt an ecumenical vision. They should see themselves as serving not particular constituencies as such but the worldwide church. Their primary allegiance should be to the gospel, not to the particular traditions they represent. Their overriding concern should be neither their own survival nor their expansion but the triumph of the kingdom of God. By being willing to die for the sake of the gospel, seminaries might insure their permanent contribution to the churches they serve. This willingness to put Christ and his kingdom before institutional survival is manifested in the courage to confess the faith in the language of the day but in contradistinction to the spirit of the times (*Zeitgeist*).

The demise of confessionalism is accompanied by a corresponding rise in ecclesiasticism in most churches and seminaries today. Loyalty to the directives of the denominational bureaucracy rather than fidelity to the confessional standards associated with the origin of their respective denominations has come to characterize a growing number of theological schools. Fundamentalist and conservative evangelical bodies have taken refuge in sectarian statements of faith that isolate the church from the critical spiritual and social issues of the time rather than bringing it into engagement with these issues.

RECOVERY OF EVANGELICAL FAITH

In order to regain their role as prophetic critics of both church and culture, theological seminaries need to reaffirm and strengthen their evangelical commitment, their devotion to the gospel of the cross. They should see their confessions of faith as being under the Bible. Their goal should be not simply the training of students for the professional ministry or priesthood but the apostolate to the nations.

I concur with Forsyth's poignant perception that there is but one way of recovering the vision and reality of a vital church: "It is by regaining, on a scale worthy of it, the evangelical faith which made and makes the Church always."[2] By "the evangelical faith" Forsyth meant the historic Christian faith, the faith grounded in the apostolic witness, reaffirmed by Augustine in his battle with Pelagius, and rediscovered by the Reformers and the Puritans. Such an evangelicalism must be clearly distinguished from the ideological or cultural evangelicalism that is so pervasive in America today.[3]

One reason why our theological seminaries are failing and why the pulpits, especially of the mainline churches, now generally give an uncertain sound (cf. 1 Cor. 14:8 KJV) is that we have lost contact with the theological and spiritual heritage of the church universal. The Bible is an addendum rather than the source and criterion of truth; the church fathers are to be listened to only where their insights tally with modern thought; religious experience is accorded a higher value than divine revelation.

Bernard Ramm makes the astute observation that most liberal preaching today is rooted in the Enlightenment rather than the Reformation and therefore takes the form of practical moral instruction rather than the announcement of a divine intervention into history that has literally changed the world.[4] I would add that this is also true of much conservative preaching, which often consists in a discourse on social problems or world events that are invariably related in a less-than-convincing way to biblical prophecy. Only rarely is there a conscientious wrestling with the text of Scripture in order to find and hear the Word of God for our time.

Theological seminaries, if they are to resist the lure of the technological society, will have to stress the rediscovery of the historical roots of the faith over communication skills and church growth strategies. In a climate in which the theological enterprise has become all too often "a *Kunstlehre,* a technology,"[5] they will have to muster the courage to give priority to content over methodology. Failure to respond to this challenge will unleash on the long-suffering local parishes a generation of technocrats with all the spiritual warmth and fervor of a computer. Logos and praxis must always be held in balance, and the same can be said for doxa (worship) and dogma.

Since the mid-1970s, the emphasis in many schools of theology has been on the renewal of worship and devotion. Spiritual formation is the latest fashion, especially in the schools of the mainline churches. Yet spirituality is no more immune to secularization than any other area of the seminary curriculum. If spirituality begins to focus on the journey inward, on realizing our inner potential, then it is clearly another betrayal of the evangelical catholic faith. There can be no vital spirituality without a sound theology. There can be no worship that is done in spirit and in truth without a certain degree of doctrinal consensus concerning the meaning of the gospel and the authority of the Bible.

We should also keep in mind that the cultivation of spirituality and the awakening to faith are two different things. Ellul calls into radical question the popular notion that spiritual exercises can eventuate in faith: "There is no path leading from a little bit of religion (of whatever kind) to a little more and finally to faith. Faith shatters all religion and everything spiritual."[6]

Notwithstanding the immense hurdles to be overcome, it is imperative that the church as well as the seminaries

strive to fulfill our Lord's earnest prayer and desire that his
people be one (John 17:20–23). Only a united church can
successfully withstand the onslaughts of secularism and
nihilism. Sectarianism is as great a sin as eclecticism and
syncretism. We need to recover the catholicity of the
church as well as its evangelistic mandate.

A genuinely catholic church will seek to be as inclusive as possible—where the demands of the gospel permit.
It will not bar from its membership any people on the
grounds of race, class, clan, or sex, nor will it treat as
inferiors any of its members for such reasons. It will also
resist the temptation to expel from its fellowship any
persons who, while holding views that may be theologically peculiar, still maintain allegiance to the gospel and the
total biblical witness to this gospel.[7] On the other hand, a
church truly catholic, evangelical, and Reformed will not
try to avoid sectarianism at any cost. Unity must never be
sought at the price of compromising and diluting the claims
of faith. The viper of compromise is even more deadly than
the contagion of sectarianism,[8] and mainline Christianity,
both Catholic and Protestant, desperately needs to face this
fact lest its salt lose its savor and worldliness triumph in
the guise of church consolidation.

DIASTASIS OR CORRELATION?

Worldliness was the issue in one of the raging controver-
sies within Protestantism from the 1930s to the early 1950s.
The question was whether the church should seek to
maintain a distance (*diastasis*) from cultural movements or
engage in dialogue with these movements so that the
creative questions of the culture are answered by the
Christian revelation. Karl Barth is associated with the first
position and Paul Tillich with the second.[9]

Both Barth and Tillich acknowledged that Christianity
has a worldly dimension. For Barth, Jesus Christ, the Son
of God, entered into this world of brokenness and despair
and identified himself with our afflictions and needs. For

Tillich, the abysmal reality that is called God is discovered precisely in the depths of the world's turmoils and discords. At the same time, both theologians were opposed to a false this-worldliness that excludes any appeal to transcendence. The problem was: Did the apologetic approach espoused by Tillich and by other existentialist theologians like Bultmann and Rahner in fact promote such a false worldliness by compromising the particularistic claims of the gospel?

The theological methods of these men differed considerably. Tillich called his approach "the method of *correlation* :" Culture is the point of departure, but the goal is revelation.[10] Barth, by contrast, believed that the only way to penetrate the enclave of culture is by kerygmatic proclamation, since the gospel carries within itself the power to persuade and convict. Tillich adopted an apologetic strategy based on common ground held with the secular culture. For Barth, it is impermissible to posit a common ground between the message of faith and the philosophical world view (*Weltanschauung*) of secular culture. The Holy Spirit must create his own point of contact, which means that not only faith but the very condition to receive faith is a gift from God. Tillich believed that we can prepare the way for the reception of faith, though faith itself must finally come from God.

A third approach is that of *identity*: here we seek a convergence between the highest values of the culture and the truth of faith. Schleiermacher and his liberal descendants (including the German Christians) have taken this position. The question can be raised whether correlation does not finally end in identity. Tillich himself acknowledged that self-discovery is tantamount to God-discovery. He was at one with Schleiermacher in the attempt to make the Christian faith palatable to its cultured despisers.[11]

Despite their theological affinities with the neoorthodoxy of Karl Barth, both Reinhold Niebuhr and Emil Brunner were closer to Tillich in the area of apologetics.[12]

They, too, began with the searchings and problems of the culture and then tried to relate these to the message of faith. They acknowledged a point of contact between the Word of God and man's self-understanding but regarded this as basically a point of conflict. The goal was to expose the deficiencies and contradictions in systems of unbelief and thereby open the door to faith in the transcendent God. The way to faith lies through "creative despair," as Niebuhr phrased it. Like Tillich they viewed the law, which convicts us of our sin and helplessness, as prior to the gospel with its promise of grace and mercy. Barth, on the other hand, regarded the gospel as prior to the law. We cannot really know the depth of our predicament until we have first been exposed to the promise of God's grace revealed in Jesus Christ. We do not really know our sin and guilt except in the light of the cross of Christ.

In an age in which secular values are so pervasive and threaten the very integrity of the faith, we need, in my opinion, to uphold the way of diastasis over both correlation and identity. Before the church can make an impact on the culture, it must break with the idolatries and misconceptions that dominate the culture. The way of diastasis should always be the way of theology, but this seems especially necessary today when the church is being infiltrated by secularism. In areas of the world where Christians are under persecution, diastasis becomes the natural strategy for the church. In America, on the other hand, where secularism so often dons the guise of religiosity, the primary danger is not persecution by the culture but seduction. Here the argument for diastasis becomes all the stronger.

Yet diastasis cannot stand by itself. The Christ-against-culture position must be held in balance with the Christ-transforming-culture position.[13] The Christian mandate is to disengage ourselves from the cultural mainstream and maintain our distance from it—but only for the purpose of returning to the arena of culture with a message that stands in judgment over its idolatries. Separation from the false values of the culture is only the first step. The conversion of the values of the culture, the transformation of its spiritual vision—this is our ultimate goal as Christians.

We live in two cities, the city of God and the city of the world (Augustine). The two are in dire conflict, but the city of the world is destined to be taken up into the city of God (Rev. 11:15), for Christ's kingdom will be triumphant over the kingdoms of this world. Yet this will not happen without conversion and much purification. The values and hopes of the world are both fulfilled and negated by the vision of a new world in Jesus Christ. The broken truths of worldly philosophy will be made to serve the fulness of truth embodied in Jesus Christ.

I do not deny that culture, even a secularized culture, still reflects the goodness and glory of God. Yet it is impossible to appreciate what is true and valid in cultural philosophy and ideology except in the light of God's self-revelation in Jesus Christ. Only in his light can we see light in nature and in culture (Ps. 36:9).

The lesson for churches and seminaries is that the key to the penetration of culture lies not in accommodation to its values or correlation with its questions. The key lies in maintaining the integrity of the gospel and the stringent demands of the law[14] in a climate of pluralism and latitudinarianism. Once we surrender the scandal of particularity, the message that God became man only at one point in history, we have lost forever the opportunity to gain a hearing in the culture. The culture will not listen to a church that is unsure of its own witness, that is willing to compromise its integrity. The church will never master the world until it breaks with the confusion and vacillation that reign in the world. The church will never include the world until it excludes the misconceptions that hold the world in bondage. By reaffirming its evangelical foundations, the church could become truly catholic in the sense of being worldwide in its outreach and impact.

IX
Human Folly and Divine Grace

And he said to me, "Son of man, can these bones live?"
And I answered, "O Lord God, thou knowest."

EZEKIEL 37:3 (RSV)

It is not help that either the Church or the world needs
most. It is power. It is life. It is moral regeneration.

P. T. FORSYTH

There is no other way to quench the thirst, to end the
drought, than through God pouring out his Spirit. There
are many in this day and age who no longer want to
believe this. Why? Because this would be something
out of the ordinary, not fitting into the usual courses of
this world.

JOHANN CHRISTOPH BLUMHARDT

THE INDEFECTIBILITY OF THE CHURCH

From the purely historical or sociological point of view, the
church faces a bleak future. Secularism seems to be
triumphant everywhere. But theologians, unlike scientific
historians, try to see reality in the light of God's self-
revelation in Jesus Christ. They know on the basis of the
biblical testimony that the powers of sin, death, and hell
have already been conquered. The demonic forces have
been dethroned, and Jesus Christ is already Lord of the
world (Col. 2:10; Eph. 1:20–23). Yet his lordship is not
universally acknowledged, and this accounts for the discord and enmity between people and nations. The demonic powers have been mortally wounded, but they still
possess the capacity to deceive. Basically, they have been
shorn of their power, but by their uncanny ability to inspire

fear and foster illusion they still hold the greater part of humanity in captivity (cf. Eph. 2:2; Rev. 12:12).

Scripture tells us that even in the midst of persecution and tribulation the holy catholic church will persevere and overcome. Various denominations or branches of the church may wither away and die, but the true church of God is indefectible. It can never be defeated, because its Lord and head, Jesus Christ, is none other than the living God. When our Lord declared that "the gates of hell shall not prevail" against his church (Matt. 16:18 KJV), he was picturing the church on the offensive against the principalities and powers of the world.

In our weakness and folly we tend to place our reliance on gimmicks and programs, on techniques that can be verified empirically, rather than on Jesus Christ himself and the gift of his Spirit to the church. There is reason for hope because time and again God's grace shatters our crutches and breaks through our defenses, which betray our lack of faith in the divine promises. We believe that a strong military defense will insure the survival of Christian civilization, whereas God can keep his church alive and even vigorous in the midst of social and political upheaval. Or we tend to think that organic mergers are the only way to maintain the efficiency of the church in a technological age. The reality of the situation is that churches that place their trust in the sword of the Spirit, the Word of God, without regard to institutional survival, including bureaucratic controls and elaborate pension schemes, will be blessed by the Spirit of God and flourish, even though this may confound management and church growth experts.

THE OUTPOURING OF THE SPIRIT

On the basis of biblical prophecy, our Puritan forebears looked forward to a latter-day outpouring of the Holy Spirit, when the church would witness new breakthroughs in Christian mission, when the gospel would be proclaimed to every nation. A church under the cross of persecution will emerge triumphant through revival, which has its roots not in new techniques of communication but in the initiative of the Holy Spirit. Even while the churches in Western Europe seem to be faltering and declining, the holy catholic church is making untold gains in the countries of the Third World, including Latin America, Africa, and Southeast Asia. Even while religiosity appears to be triumphing over biblical faith in America, the wind of the Spirit is moving among groups and communities that are curtly dismissed by mainline Protestant as well as establishment evangelical churches as reflecting a naive folk piety.

This brings to mind the parable of the marriage feast (Matt. 22:1–14; Luke 14:16–24). When those who are formally invited fail to respond, others will be invited to celebrate the victory of Christ and the rapture of the church. If the privileged peoples of Western Europe and America close their ears to the divine promise and the divine imperative, then the Spirit will take the Word of God to others, to the poor and forsaken who have been relegated to the marginal areas of society—both in the West and in the Third World. Jesus himself declared that he had come not to call the righteous to repentance but sinners (Matt. 9:13; Lk. 5:32). Those who pretend to see will be made blind, but those who acknowledge their blindness and helplessness will be made to see (John 9:39). The door will finally be closed to the privileged (both in the spiritual and in the political sense), but those who recognize and deplore their spiritual poverty will be welcomed into the fellowship of the kingdom. The sons of the kingdom will be thrown into the outer darkness, but penitent sinners will be given a share in the glory of paradise (Matt. 8:5–12; 22:1–14; 24:45–51; 25:14–30; Luke 13:22–30).

AN APOCALYPTIC AGE

Today the foundations of civilization are being shaken as
never before (cf. Ps. 11:3; Isa. 14:16–17; 24:18–19; 64:2).
The old order is crumbling as the powers of darkness
prepare to make their final stand. The shadow of persecution is falling upon the church, but as Christians we have
the assurance that through perseverance and martyrdom
victory will be secured. When worldliness enters the
church, when false prophets appear on the scene, the time
is ripe for the birth of a confessing church that crosses all
denominational lines. A church that confesses the Word of
God in all of its power and glory, that affirms the whole
gospel and not simply a segment of the gospel, will
certainly meet with severe opposition, even outright persecution. But the blood of the martyrs is the seed of the
church (Tertullian), and this means that the latter-day
revival will probably come through a church engaged in a
relentless battle to maintain its identity and remain true to
its mission. It is a church poignantly aware that the victory
is secure, because it knows that the final outcome has
already been decided by the cross and resurrection victory
of Jesus Christ. V-Day (the Day of Victory) already looms
on the horizon because D-Day (the Day of the Decisive
Battle) has already occurred.[1]

In the apocalyptic age in which we are living, when
the forces of evil seem so pervasive, when divine intervention alone can empower the church as well as redeem the
world, the books of Daniel and Revelation become especially relevant.[2] The beast of the abyss, the anti-Christ, the
abomination of desolation, all these symbols of radical evil
will make one last desperate attempt to regain a torn world
reclaimed by Jesus Christ. But both of these biblical books
also speak of the coming again of Jesus Christ to confirm
and reveal to the whole creation his cross and resurrection
victory. In addition, the Book of Revelation envisions a
period of millennial glory, prior to the final consummation

when there will be a new heaven and a new earth and God will be all in all. The church today needs to reincorporate the millennial hope, the confident expectation that the kingdom of God will be realized on earth as well as in heaven. Even under persecution, the church should hold out hope for the earth as well as for the elect of God. Some of God's promises will be realized not only beyond history but also in worldly history.

With the emergence of a monolithic state that seeks all power for itself, the church is called to rethink the implications of Romans 13 where Paul commands respect and honor for the state. But in interpreting these passages, we must not confuse the state with the nation. Government as such should always be given respect by the community of the faithful, for otherwise society could fall into anarchy. But respect for government should not be confused with veneration of the nation or people (*das Volk*) who represent a particular cultural and ethnic heritage. Nationalism and racism are modern idolatries, and when the state is made to serve the aspirations of race or nation instead of the cause of justice for all, it becomes a demonic state warranting resistance and rejection by the Christian faithful (cf. Rev. 13).[3]

As Christians, Catholic and Protestant, we can face the future with hope and confidence. Even if the institutional churches should collapse, the holy catholic church will live on and go from victory to victory. The gospel cannot be defeated, for its victory has already been secured. Jesus Christ has truly conquered the powers of death and destruction. The reverberations of his great victory are still to be felt and appreciated by the whole of creation. What he has done on behalf of all is still to be revealed for all to discern, but it cannot be controverted or reversed.

The proper stance of the Christian in these last days, when the devil is let loose to cause ravage and destruction, to test and thereby purify the ranks of the faithful (2 Thess. 2:3, 4; Rev. 20:3), is a provisional pessimism but an ultimate optimism. Through trial and tribulation the church will endure and emerge as the only kingdom with power and authority. Every knee shall bow and every tongue shall confess that Jesus is Lord (Phil. 2:10, 11), but only those who have remained true to the end will make this confession as his sons and daughters, as the company of the redeemed.

REDISCOVERING THE SPIRITUAL GIFTS

Christians can only live out their vocation by discovering and exercising the gifts of the Holy Spirit. Indeed, these gifts were bestowed primarily to enable members of the body of Christ to be his witnesses and ambassadors.

Are some gifts more important than others in our time? Certainly it behooves us to give more attention to the role of teaching. When false prophets abound and occultism is rampant, we need people who will give instruction in sound doctrine—not only clergy but also laity. The charisms of preaching, evangelism, leadership, and discernment of spirits also have special value for our age. Probably most of us know churches or religious institutions that are teetering on the brink of disaster or have already gone over the edge because their leaders lacked these last two gifts. Likewise, the word of wisdom and the word of knowledge should earnestly be sought if the church is to give proper spiritual direction, a pastoral care that is grounded in the gospel rather than in the social sciences or the cult of narcissism. Prophecy is also important if the church is to find its way through the current darkness, for its leaders are already being compelled to make decisions that could shape the future of any given congregation.

There is one additional gift that has crucial significance for our time, one not mentioned specifically in the New Testament but alluded to in both Testaments: the gift of battle (cf. Deut. 31:6; Josh. 1:6–9; 2 Sam. 10:12; Dan. 10:19; Acts 23:11; 1 Cor. 16:13; Eph. 6:10–17;

1 Thess. 2: 2; 1 Tim. 6:12). Moses was engaged in spiritual battle when he came down from Mount Sinai and had to deal with the abominable idolatry of his people (Exod. 32). Christians who are under the cross of persecution need to pray for the gift of battle, the ability to endure under trial, the boldness to challenge immorality and heresy in high places. The gift of battle is properly included in the gift of might or power (Isa. 11:2). It is the power to enter into conflict and the stamina not to grow weary. It must be accompanied by and fulfilled in the gift of love, since we cannot wage war against sin successfully unless we love the sinner. We must speak the truth, but we must speak the truth in love.

Christians who enter the battle against the powers of darkness cannot persevere without a life-support system, without a supportive fellowship that continually holds up its members in intercession to the living God. Moses was not able to challenge Pharaoh apart from the support of Aaron. Nor could he prevail in prayer without the aid of Aaron and Hur when the children of Israel were engaged in combat with the Amalekites (Exod. 17:8–13). Were it not for the invisible support of the angelic hosts, Elisha could not have stood up against the Syrians (2 Kings 6:15–17).

Most of us resemble Elijah, who fled into the wilderness rather than confronting the priests of Baal, or Jonah, who sought to evade the divine commandment to preach repentance to the people of Nineveh. Christoph Blumhardt laments that there is often *"only a very small band of those who* truly want to be *fighters."* [4] Even among Christians, he says, it is rare to find a single person who is willing to do battle for the gospel. "They will not give their lives even unto death; and whoever will not do so can never be a disciple of Jesus, fighting for his victory."[5]

THE HOPE OF THE CHURCH

It is important to remember, however, that Jesus Christ does not need our aid in the completion of his mission. He does not really need the church, but he has created the church for the purpose of preparing the way for the coming kingdom. He wishes to enlist us in his service, but he has the capacity to raise sons of Abraham out of stones (Matt. 3:9). He can plead his own cause (Ps. 74:22), but we can bear witness to his apologetic. We can be instruments of his grace, but he may choose to use other instruments, or he may bestow his grace directly. When we conquer, it is he who is conquering in and through us. When we fail, he may be withdrawing his grace from us in order to test us or to chastise us for our disobedience.

The coming of the kingdom rests upon his decision. He will select the time and the means. We cannot bring in the kingdom, but we can manifest the present reality of the kingdom by the power of his Spirit. We cannot build the kingdom, but we can herald and proclaim it. We can be stewards of the mystery of the gospel, but we cannot make the gospel successful. The gospel makes its own way in the world, for it is the very word of the all-powerful Son of God, Lord of the universe, Savior of humankind. But Christ has indicated that he wishes to speak his word through our broken words. It is through the folly of what we preach that Christ saves those who believe (cf. 1 Cor. 1:21; Rom. 10:17). But when he uses us as his heralds and instruments, he often speaks against our words as well as through them, over them as well as in them.

We can be servants of the gospel but not masters. We can be signs of grace but not dispensers of grace. The surest way to combat the ideology of the technological society is to surrender any pretension that we can make the gospel relevant or credible to its cultured despisers. We can discover the relevance that is already in the gospel, but even this discovery must be attributed to the grace of God, certainly not to human ingenuity.

The hope of the church rests on its Lord who will never let his children be snatched from his hand (John 10:29), who not only draws us into the kingdom but makes us servants of the kingdom. We are not only saved by grace but also kept by grace. At the same time, we must give evidence to the world that our state of grace is genuine. We must let our light shine so that people will see our good works and give glory to the Father who is in heaven (Matt. 5:16). Christ alone is the light, but we can be light-bearers. He alone is the Savior, but we can be covenant partners with him in making his salvation manifest to a world lost in confusion and despair. The light shines in the darkness, and the darkness will not be able to overcome it (John 1:5). This is our hope, and even if the institutional churches should crumble and fall, the kingdom of Christ will go from victory to victory.

Because *Jesus is Victor* (Johann Christoph Blumhardt), we can face the future with confidence and hope—even a future under the shadow of nuclear war, even a future that might very well entail untold tribulation for the church. Let us rejoice, because the old age is passing away. The Word of God has become flesh, and his glory is destined to fill the whole earth (Ps. 72:19; Isa. 52:10; 66:18; Hab. 2:14).

X
Discipleship Under
the Cross

"How long will you falter between two opinions? If the Lord is God, follow Him; but if Baal, then follow him."

1 KINGS 18:21 (NKJV)

When principles that run against your deepest convictions begin to win the day, then battle is your calling, and peace has become sin; you must, at the price of dearest peace, lay your convictions bare before friend and enemy, with all the fire of your faith.

ABRAHAM KUYPER

If the world has not come to its end, it has approached a major turn in history, equal in importance to the turn from the Middle Ages to the Renaissance. It will exact from us a spiritual upsurge, we shall have to rise to a new height of vision, to a new level of life where our physical nature will not be cursed as in the Middle Ages, but, even more importantly, our spiritual being will not be trampled upon as in the modern era.

ALEXANDER SOLZHENITSYN

THE CALL TO OBEDIENCE

Our hope is in Jesus Christ alone, but this should not be taken as a pretext for quietism. We are challenged to live according to this hope. We are called to acts of sacrificial love·on behalf of the oppressed and despairing in the light of his victory. Our mandate is to carry this victory forward in the world in the power and illumination that come to us from his Spirit.

Only his cross atones for sin, but he bids us take up our cross in lowly discipleship and follow him (Matt. 16:24). Obedience to the divine commandment is the way in which we manifest the fruits of his victory in the world. Our cross functions as a witness and sign of his cross.

The Christian mandate is not simply to turn away from the evil that surrounds us, in the manner of the proverbial monkeys of Buddhist piety who close their ears and eyes to all discord and rancor. Our task is to combat the evil weighing down upon us in the power of the Spirit. We are called to be the light of the world, the leaven in the lump, the salt of the earth (Matt. 5:13, 14; 1 Cor. 5:6–7). We can only be light, leaven, and salt by working within the structures of society, bringing them into subjection to the Lord, "who is God over all" (Rom. 9: 5 NIV).

If, out of fearfulness or weariness, we withdraw from the political and cultural arena into private citadels of righteousness, it may mean that we have given up the battle and have abandoned the world to the devil. On the other hand, a certain kind of withdrawal is permissible and in some cases even mandatory if its purpose is eventual return to continue the battle on a deeper level.

Active obedience under the cross is the very opposite of mindless activism in which we let the world dictate our agenda. Productivity and efficiency are the virtues of the technological society, but they are not necessarily Christian virtues. What is needed is contact with the wellsprings of our faith if we are to be a transforming influence in the world. Creative action has its roots in contemplation— prayer, study, and disciplined reflection on the revelation of God in Jesus Christ. We are obliged to practice creative disaffiliation from the demands of the world in order to be free for creative involvement in the pressing needs of the world. We should likewise detach ourselves as much as possible from the sinful illusions of the world in order to identify with the plight of the victims of these illusions.[1]

It is important to bear in mind that our obedience is to be measured not by tangible results (the criterion of the technological society) but instead by fidelity to the divine commandment. When someone asked Mother Teresa, founder of the Missionaries of Charity, how she could continue her battle against poverty in India when there seemed so little likelihood of succeeding, she replied with the wisdom that comes from being close to God: "We are not called to be successful; we are called to be faithful."

Our ministry to persons is based on their election by God's incomparable love, not on their possible contribution to a better society. As Christians, we basically see other people not in terms of their function in the social order but in terms of their relationship to God. I reject Whitehead's maxim that "a thing *is* what it *does*."[2] On the contrary, I would argue that our identity is based on what has been done for us by God in Jesus Christ.

THE FORMS OF OUR OBEDIENCE

As disciples under the cross, we are first of all to be obedient to the great commission—to proclaim the gospel to the whole creation (Mark 16: 15; Matt. 28:18–20). This is the apostolic or evangelistic mandate of the church, what Roman Catholics refer to as "the apostolate of souls." General William Booth, founder of the Salvation Army, had his priorities right when he told those under his command: "Go for souls—and go for the worst."

The apostolic mission of the church involves not only proclamation (*kerygma*) but also training in discipleship (*didache*). This training, however, is not simply for spiritual growth but for evangelistic outreach. The key to peace among the nations is the conversion of the human spirit. The heart of stone must be replaced by a heart of flesh (Ezek. 11: 19; 36: 26). It is the Spirit of the living God, moreover, working through our preaching, who alone regenerates the human heart, bringing to people a new motivation and a new goal in life.

But evangelism, however crucial, does not cover the full range of our responsibilities. Works of mercy must be high on our agenda. We are obliged not only to present the invitation of the gospel but also to practice the imperatives of the gospel: feeding the hungry, clothing the naked, ministering to the sick, visiting those in prison, caring for the aged (Isa. 58:7; Matt. 25:31–46; Luke 10:25–37; 1 Tim. 5:1–8; Rom. 12:20; James 1:27; 2:15–16). Our motivation for these works of mercy is love, but our goal is evangelism—bringing all people into a right relationship with God. We are not truly serving humanity unless we seek to meet spiritual as well as material needs. Until there is a change of heart, we are only building people up to destroy one another.[3] As Teresa of Avila so aptly put it, "The soul of the care of the poor is the care of the poor soul." Works of mercy constitute the service mandate of the church (*diakonia*).

The people of God are also required to do works of justice (cf. Ps. 82:3–4; Amos 5:21–24; Isa 58:6; 61:1, 8). It is not enough to minister to personal needs. We must act to alleviate or drastically alter the appalling social conditions that aggravate these needs, that accentuate the misery and poverty that are part of the human condition. This is the political mandate of the church. The church fulfills this mandate by bringing the law of God to bear on the critical moral issues of the time in its proclamation and teaching, issues such as abortion, the nuclear armaments race, the breakdown of the family, environmental pollution, and the growing disparity between rich and poor. It also obeys this injunction when it encourages its members as citizens of the state to press for legislation that will humanize oppressive social structures. It is not the renunciation of power but the right use of power that brings society into greater conformity with the law of God.

In this area of political engagement, we need to be on guard against two perennial temptations. The first is to align ourselves with a cultural ideology in order to reach the goal of greater justice for all peoples. The message of the church then becomes confused with a political platform, and the blessed hope is reduced to a utopian vision.

We must always be mindful of the infinite qualitative difference between the transcendent claims of the gospel and the dictates of an ideological system, which invariably distorts reality by its blind adherence to the interests of a particular class in society. The second temptation is closely related: the vain expectation that our political and social reforms will inaugurate the kingdom of God.[4] Political reforms may produce a more equitable society but not necessarily a more loving one. They can put bandages on wounds, but they cannot heal the infection of sin, the source of human misery. Not until a new kind of man is created will the kingdom of God be present, and only the Spirit of God can bring about this regenerative work.[5]

Evangelical Christianity unashamedly contends that the key to social reformation is personal regeneration. We begin with the interior change and then proceed outward to the complexities and intricacies of social relationships. The love of God that comes to us in the moment of decision awakens within us a corresponding love for our neighbor. We are thus moved to enter into the social conflicts of the time, fired by a desire to glorify God in the depths of the world's despair and also by a compassionate concern for an oppressed and beleaguered humanity.

If our striving for social righteousness is motivated by faith, hope, and love, it can itself be a powerful witness to the coming kingdom of God. The justice that we can achieve on earth must never be identified with the higher righteousness of the kingdom, but it can call attention to this righteousness by creating a thirst for it.

Our commitment to social justice will be self-defeating if it is not grounded in works of piety, which serve to deepen our relationship with God: worship, prayer, meditation, devotional reading, fasting. Indeed, works of piety comprise a crucial dimension of the spiritual mandate of the church (which also includes evangelism and confession) as opposed to its cultural mandate (works of mercy and justice). Thomas Aquinas rightly contended that works of piety have a certain priority over works of mercy, although the two must always go hand in hand.

We often fail to realize that the hardest work of all is prayer, since it means humbly acknowledging that only God can accomplish lasting social and spiritual change and that our primary task is to place ourselves at his disposal. All creative action in the world (mission, service, social reform) is ultimately grounded in the discipline of prayer— adoration, thanksgiving, personal petition, and interces- sion. Prayer is an arduous task, but it is at the same time a gift from God, for we could not pray in the power of the Spirit unless the Spirit were acting upon us and with us (cf. Rom. 8:15–16, 23, 26–27).

Biblical prayer requires a humble heart and a mind awake (Col. 4:2–6 NEB). But our mental activity should not stop there. We need to apply ourselves to the work of theology, which enables the church to give a sound and clear exposition of its faith to both the people of God and the outside world (2 Cor. 11:4–6; 2 Tim. 1:11; 4:2–4; Titus 1:9,13,14; 2:1,15). This discipline provides the church with the intellectual tools to combat heresy from within and paganism from without. It involves diligent study of the biblical Word as well as of the world in the light of this Word, but always for the purpose of rendering an intelligible and faithful witness. The theological task is motivated by a concern for the integrity of the church's witness as the church seeks to maintain its identity in a culture that is often hostile to the claims of the gospel. Thus the vocation to theology, which is in the service of both nurture and evangelism, is to be subsumed under the confessional mandate of the church.

Not all Christians, of course, can be professional theologians (teachers), just as we cannot all be evangelists, pastors, healers, social workers, monks, or nuns. The reason is that God bestows different gifts for various forms of ministry (1 Cor. 12:4–31). But it behooves all of us who take up the cross of discipleship to reflect on our faith and to confess our faith in words as well as in deeds. Faith only becomes strong when it is confessed, and it becomes weak when those who profess it let themselves be intimidated into silence by an unfriendly world.

We may well be entering a new church struggle (*Kirchenkampf*) in which the fundamentals of the faith are increasingly called into question. Purity of doctrine is as essential as purity in worship. In fact, the reason for the erosion of a biblical spirituality today is the erosion of the apostolic and doctrinal substance of the faith. Right worship (doxa) is grounded in right doctrine (dogma). But right doctrine cannot be maintained apart from the practice of the spiritual life. Only theologians in daily contact with the Spirit of God can successfully discriminate between truth and error and thereby produce sound theology.

In our time, I have suggested, a confessing church is likely to become a church under the cross of persecution. Christians who are bold to confess their faith in the face of the principalities and powers of the age may well end up as martyrs. Yet the church lives and thrives on the afflictions of its confessors and martyrs, and this is not a reason for despair but for hope.

DISCIPLESHIP AS A SIGN OF REDEMPTION

We must not be beguiled into believing that living out the demands of costly discipleship can actually procure either our justification or our sanctification. Nor can it bring about the sanctification of the social order, which is a special work of divine grace. But our works of love and mercy can manifest and demonstrate the justification and sanctification that Christ has already won for us. They can also contribute to the humanization of the social order and so bear witness to the sanctifying work of the Spirit as he extends the kingdom of God in the world today.

We sow the seed, but he brings the fruit. We can prepare the way, but he sets the time. The present is under his control, and the future is in his hands. The fulfillment of time (the *kairos*) has already occurred, but the consummation of time (the *parousia*) is still to come. Our task is to bear witness to both of these events as we live out the destiny that heaven has in store for us between the times.

Far from inducing resignation to the order of things, this biblical vision spurs us to works of mercy and justice, because we know that the enemy has already been mortally defeated. Such a vision gives us a holy optimism that fortifies us for the battles that are already descending upon us. It is a paradoxical but verifiable truth that a vital belief in divine predestination is the source of creative, transforming action in the world. This is a predestination that is realized through the obedience of faith and also, mysterious as it may seem, through the folly of unbelief.

In our vanity, we tend to forget that we are not the author of salvation but rather its heralds and emissaries. We are all too ready to believe that the future is not in God's hands but in ours. We fondly imagine that our feeble witness can actually accomplish what he has promised to do by his Spirit. What our witness does accomplish is to remind people that God is already at work making all things new. And now and again he works in conjunction with our witness, reaching people and turning them toward the cross of Christ in repentance and faith.

Scripture tells us that through our prayers, witness, and godly life we can hasten the day of the Lord (2 Peter 3:11–12; Acts 3:19–21), though we cannot force the hand of God. When we realize our vocation as heralds and ambassadors of Jesus Christ, we are bringing the great commission closer to fulfillment, and this means that the day of the Lord is also approaching (Matt. 24: 14). We can be instruments of the Spirit in the final ingathering of the harvest of souls (Matt. 9:37–38; Luke 10:2; Jn. 4:35), but it is God himself who will usher in the dramatic consummation of world history when "the sovereignty of the world" will pass "to our Lord and his Christ" (Rev. 11:15 NEB).

As we reflect on the dreadful things that are happening today—the erosion of spiritual and ethical norms, growing apostasy in the church, the proliferation of the cults, the recrudescence of nationalism and militarism—it is easy for us to become disheartened. The temptation to succumb to fear of nuclear war, of the future, of the unknown is almost irresistible. Fear is the deadly enemy of faith, for it drains the energy and weakens the resolve of even the most resilient. The antidote to fear is remembering that God has not kept silent (Ps. 50:3) but has entered into the struggle of his people for freedom and deliverance. The upheavals of our time testify to the fact that the kingdom of God is drawing near.

What is important to realize is that God himself is bringing about the moral and spiritual desolation that is rampant today. He is even at work confusing the counsel and deliberations of many of his shepherds who have proved to be unworthy witnesses (cf. 1 Kings 22:22–23; 2 Chron. 18:21–22; Isa.29:9–10,13–14; Jer. 22:22; Ezek. 14:9–10). The nations rage and the kingdoms totter (cf. Ps. 46:6 NKJV) because they stand under the wrath and judgment of a holy God. But his judgment is there precisely for our redemption and for the redemption of the nations (cf. Ezek. 36:33–36). As the Psalmist wisely observes,

> Come, behold the works of the Lord,
> Who has made desolations in the earth. . . .
> Be still, and know that I am God;
> I will be exalted among the nations,
> I will be exalted in the earth!
>
> (Ps. 46:8,19 NKJV)

Sometimes waiting for the Lord is more fruitful and rewarding than dreaming of strategies to save the world. When we wait on the Lord in prayer and penitence, believing in his promises, we will eventually hear his commandment. And then it is our task to rise and herald the good news—that Jesus Christ has come, is here now, and will come again (Rev. 1:4). Through the desolation that he has wrought, a new world will appear, and a chastened church will again begin to sing his praises.

Notes

CHAPTER ONE—INTRODUCTION

[1]Ellul is adamant that technology is not morally neutral because it invariably carries with it harmful side effects. While acknowledging that technology may have some felicitous consequences, he contends that it is at best morally ambiguous because of the enhanced possibilities for evil. Ellul is probably right that technique cannot be separated from its use, and it therefore tends to be in the service of the human lust for power. But if the Holy Spirit is a living reality in the lives of Christians, may not technology also on occasion serve the desire to glorify God? See Jacques Ellul, *The Technological Society*, trans. John Wilkinson (New York: Vintage Books, 1964), esp. pp. 96–98. It should be noted that Ellul does not suggest that we abandon technology but that we demythologize it.

[2]Reinhold Niebuhr, *Moral Man and Immoral Society* (New York: Scribner's, 1932), 24.

[3]According to Rousseau and Dewey, the common good is best served by fidelity to the general will or the cause of social unification.

[4]Vernard Eller, *Towering Babble* (Elgin, Ill.: Brethren Press, 1983), 41–52.

[5]This criticism may be slightly harsh in light of the fact that the Fourteenth General Synod of the United Church of Christ authorized a Pentecost peace offering in 1984 and 1985. Yet in my perusal of UCC peace literature I do not find the penultimate quest for worldly peace effectively related to the ultimate concern for peace with God through faith in Jesus Christ.

[6]*The Challenge of Peace: God's Promise and Our Response* (Washington, D.C.: United States Catholic Conference, 1983), 88. The Bishops' Pastoral Letter is not exempt from a certain kind of romantic idealism that sees "love" as "the only real hope for all human relations" (p. 25). For my critique of the Catholic Bishops' statement, see Donald G. Bloesch, "The Catholic Bishops on War and Peace," *Center Journal* 3 (Winter 1983): 163–76.

[7]Even many of the new breakaway groups are eager for cooperation with fellow believers in evangelism and social service.

CHAPTER TWO—DEATH AND RESURRECTION

[1]See John Shelton Curtiss, *The Russian Church and the Soviet State* (Boston: Little, Brown, 1953), 112–20. Patriarch Tikhon was quoted as saying that it was the government's concern, not the church's, to care for those dying of starvation (p. 120). It is well to bear in mind that many Russian Orthodox priests as well as their parishioners did not follow the

Patriarch's lead and did use church valuables to provide for famine relief. It should also be recognized that Patriarch Tikhon at one point favored donations of nonconsecrated articles to the poor.

The antipathy of the Communists toward Patriarch Tikhon was ultimately based not on his adherence to church rule on the matter of vestments and other church treasures, but on the fact that he was a sign of transcendence which they felt obliged to eradicate.

[2]This assessment is given a measure of support by Bernard Semmel, *The Methodist Revolution* (New York: Basic Books, 1973); and J. Wesley Bready, *England Before and After Wesley: The Evangelical Revival and Social Reform* (London: Hodder & Stoughton, 1939). Bready declares: "The Revival's character-building influence provided the solid foundation upon which the social and industrial emancipation of the English masses was reared, while also it gave to women their first extensive opportunities of serving the common weal" (p. 326).

[3]Bernard E. Meland, *America's Spiritual Culture* (New York: Harper & Bros., 1948), 52.

[4]See Pat Robertson's critique of George Gilder's apologia for capitalism in his book *The Secret Kingdom* (Nashville: Thomas Nelson, 1982), 151–55. Robertson argues that commitment to the law of reciprocity will advance both capitalism and evangelical Christianity.

[5]Ivan Illich, "Education: A Consumer Commodity and a Pseudo-Religion", *Christian Century* 88 (December 15, 1971): 1464.

[6]Vernard Eller, ed. *Thy Kingdom Come: A Blumhardt Reader* (Grand Rapids: Eerdmans, 1980), 144–45.

CHAPTER THREE–THE PHENOMENON OF SECULARISM

[1]Cited in William Hubben, *Dostoevsky, Kierkegaard, Nietzsche, and Kafka* (New York: Collier, 1979), 47.

[2]Reinhold Niebuhr, *Does Civilization Need Religion?* (New York: Macmillan, 1927), 67.

[3]Paul Althaus, *Die deutsche Stunde der Kirche* (Göttingen: Vandenhoeck & Ruprecht, 1933), 5. Bonino observes that though Althaus "tries to raise defenses against a paganization of the gospel, his booklet shocks by the way it gives religious sanction to 'German nationalism' without at the same time trying to bring the contents of the gospel to bear on the nature and purpose of that nationalism." José Míguez Bonino, *Toward a Christian Political Ethics* (Philadelphia: Fortress, 1983), 118. Bonino can be criticized for accommodating the gospel to the ideology of the left.

[4]Conservatives like Walther Künneth, Hans Lilje, and Karl Heim were active in the Young Reformation movement, also vehemently anti-Nazi. Friedrich von Bodelschwingh, representative of the Pietist tradition in Lutheranism, was noted for his forthright opposition to Nazism and to the German Christians.

[5]Paul Tillich, because of his commitment to religious socialism, was involved in an ideological battle with the Nazis and felt it expedient to leave Germany in 1933 to assume a post at Union Theological Seminary in New York. The following year, however, he sought to regain his

professorship in Germany by reminding the Berlin Ministry for Science, Art, and Education that certain of his theological concepts had lent themselves for use by National Socialist theoreticians. Rather than throwing his support behind the Confessing Church, he sought a third way between the German Christians and the Confessing Church, which would attract liberal Christians committed to the cause of social justice. See Wilhelm and Marion Pauck, *Paul Tillich: His Life & Thought* (New York: Harper & Row, 1976), 1: 149–50, 191–92.

Like Tillich, Rudolf Bultmann was no friend of the German Christians, openly objecting to the "Aryan paragraph," which excluded Christians of Jewish descent from holding offices in the church. At the same time, Bultmann took the oath of unconditional allegiance to Hitler, which was required of all university professors, and criticized Karl Barth for not doing so. Barth retorted that their different approaches to this political and social crisis were rooted in a different concept of Christianity. See Bernd Jaspert, ed., *Karl Barth/Rudolf Bultmann Letters 1922–1966*, Trans. & ed. Geoffrey W. Bromiley (Grand Rapids: Eerdmans, 1981), 78–80, 84.

The German Christian movement drew support from many people associated with a cultural or liberal brand of Christianity, including Emanuel Hirsch, Friedrich Wieneke, and Wilhelm Stapel. Among mediating theologians within Lutheranism who opposed the Barmen Declaration and lent support to the German Christians were Paul Althaus, Gerhard Kittel, and Friedrich Gogarten. The orthodox Lutheran Hans Asmussen, on the other hand, was an unashamed defender of the Barmen Declaration and active in the Confessing Church movement.

For the story of the Confessing Church movement see Arthur C. Cochrane, *The Church's Confession Under Hitler* (Pittsburgh: Pickwick, 1976). See also Arthur Frey, *Cross and Swastika*,trans. J. Strathearn McNab (London: Student Christian Movement, 1938); Peter Matheson, ed., *The Third Reich and the Christian Churches* (Grand Rapids: Eerdmans, 1981); and Ernst Christian Helmreich, *The German Churches Under Hitler: Background, Struggle, and Epilogue* (Detroit: Wayne State University Press, 1979).

[6]Franklin Littell, *The Crucifixion of the Jews* (New York: Harper & Row, 1975), 97.

[7]It is interesting to note that Whitehead supported Chamberlain's "accommodation" to Hitler at Munich as a step toward peace in our time. See Charles Hartshorne, *Insights and Oversights of Great Thinkers* (Albany: State University of New York Press, 1983), 321.

[8]Bernard E. Meland, *America's Spiritual Culture* (New York: Harper & Bros., 1948), 91. For a further elucidation of his position, see his *Faith and Culture* (New York: Oxford University Press, 1953).

[9]Meland, *America's Spiritual Culture*, 36. Meland goes on to assert that the primary goal of religion is to enhance "the culture of the human spirit in whatever soil human life grows" (p. 120).

[10]Ibid., 45.

[11]H. Richard Niebuhr, Wilhelm Pauck, and Francis P. Miller, *The Church Against the World* (New York: Willett, Clark, 1935).

[12]Frederick Sontag and John Roth, *The American Religious Experience* (New York: Harper & Row, 1972). Sontag is an eclectic thinker who draws upon existentialism, pragmatism, and process philosophy. In his book *The God of Evil* (New York: Harper & Row, 1970), he asserts the priority of becoming over being and makes clear that God is subject to change and suffering. He argues, moreover, that God has no choice but to create, for his nature would remain too unspecific unless he gave existence to some portion of it. In addition, this philosopher locates nonbeing in the nature of God. See pp. 138–139,159ff.

Another scholar who has called for a uniquely American theology is Herbert Richardson in his *Toward an American Theology* (New York: Harper & Row, 1967). Interestingly, both Sontag and Richardson have been remarkably open to the Unification Church movement, which contains a marked nationalistic thrust.

[13]Sontag and Roth, *The American Religious Experience*, 372.

[14]Ibid., 375.

[15]Pierre Teilhard de Chardin, *The Future of Man*, trans. Norman Denny (New York: Harper & Row, 1964), 46.

[16]Cited in Thomas Molnar, *God and the Knowledge of Reality* (New York: Basic Books, 1973), 185–86. From Teilhard de Chardin, *Sauvons l'humanité*, trans. W. H. Marshner, 1937.

[17]See Richard Lischer, "From Earth to Heaven: Teilhard's Politics and Eschatology," *Christian Century* 92 (April 9, 1975): 353.

[18]R. C. Zaehner, *Zen, Drugs and Mysticism* (New York: Pantheon Books, 1972), 172–84, 196–98; and Thomas Molnar, *God and the Knowledge of Reality*, 180–86. For a more positive but not uncritical appraisal of Teilhard's thought, see Doran McCarty, *Teilhard de Chardin* (Waco: Word, 1976).

[19]See José Miranda, *Communism in the Bible*, trans. Robert Barr (New York: Orbis, 1982); *Marx Against the Marxists: The Christian Humanism of Karl Marx*, trans. John Drury (New York: Orbis, 1980).

[20]Adolf Keller, *Religion and the European Mind* (London: Lutterworth, 1934), 113.

[21]Prominent Latin American theologians associated with liberation theology are Gustavo Gutiérrez, José Miranda, Jon Sobrino, José Míguez Bonino, and Paulo Freire.

[22]Virginia Mollenkott states the case for inclusive language for God in her book *The Divine Feminine* (New York: Crossroad, 1983). She advocates speaking of God as "Father/Mother," substituting "the Human One" for "Son of Man" and changing the last words of the Doxology to "Creator, Christ and Holy Ghost" instead of "Father, Son and Holy Ghost." With process theologian Schubert Ogden, she envisions God as "the Absolute Relatedness," a concept associated with philosophical panentheism rather than biblical theism. Mollenkott's views are typical of the prevailing feminist sentiment in the mainline Protestant denominations. While careful not to align herself with those feminists who uphold a Goddess spirituality, she is nevertheless sympathetic to their concerns. See Virginia Mollenkott, "An Evangelical Feminist Confronts the Goddess," *Christian Century* 99 (October 20, 1982): 1043–46; and her

review of Carl Olson, ed., *The Book of the Goddess, Past and Present* (New York: Crossroad, 1983) in *Christian Century* 101 (February 22, 1984): 204.

The *Inclusive Language Lectionary* issued by the National Council of Churches in October 1983 reflects the same general orientation (Mollenkott was one of the authors). God is portrayed as both Father and Mother, and such primal symbols as "Lord," "Son of God," "Son of Man," and "kingdom of God" are replaced by more "inclusive" imagery.

[23]Another example of natural theology today is black theology, which, like feminist theology, belongs within the wider movement of liberation theology, though its focus is on black self-determination and racial injustice rather than on class conflict. Black theology reconceives God as black, meaning that he fully identifies himself with the struggle for black liberation. In this perspective, the ruling norm for the interpretation of Scripture is the black experience or black consciousness. See James Cone, *A Black Theology of Liberation* (New York: Lippincott, 1970) and Albert Cleage, *Black Christian Nationalism* (New York: Morrow, 1972).

[24]It is important to differentiate between the moderate and more radical wings of "German Christianity," which was never a homogeneous movement. The moderate wing wished to retain the fundamental doctrines of the faith, including the Trinity and the deity of Jesus Christ. The radical wing saw Jesus primarily as a heroic prophetic figure and God as the spirit of the race. It was the radical element that gained ascendancy in the movement.

Likewise, we need to distinguish between the different positions within feminism. The radicals seek an immanentalistic religion, and some wish to abandon the biblical heritage altogether, which they dismiss as incurably patriarchal. More moderate elements are intent on bringing the faith into harmony with a social egalitarianism that affirms the dignity and essential independence of women. If Charlene Spretnak's *The Politics of Women's Spirituality* is representative of modern feminism, it would seem that the future belongs to those of a more radical inclination. (Charlene Spretnak, ed., *The Politics of Women's Spirituality: Essays on the Rise of Spiritual Power Within the Feminist Movement* [New York: Doubleday, 1982]).

It is also important to differentiate ideological feminism from the women's rights movement, which includes feminist ideologues but also many other women and men who seek fair employment for women in the areas of government, education, commerce, and industry. Women in academic religious circles today who affirm women's rights as well as a more visible role for women in the area of spiritual leadership but distance themselves from ideological feminism include Elizabeth Achtemeier, Old Testament scholar at Union Seminary in Richmond, Virginia; Lucetta Mowry, a member of the Revised Standard Version Bible Committee; and Marion Battles, the widow of the renowned Calvin scholar Ford Lewis Battles. Such women uphold the biblical model of the complementarity of the sexes rather than the mythical vision of androgyny, the ultimate fusion of the masculine and feminine in a higher spiritual whole, which is attractive to many ideological feminists. Mary Daly defended androgyny in her *Beyond God the Father* (Boston: Beacon,

1973), but she has now broken with this concept in favor of the lesbian ideal.

[25]Keller, *Religion and the European Mind*, 109.

[26]Paul B. Means, *Things That Are Caesar's* (New York: Round Table Press, 1935), 182-84. Cf. Ernst Christian Helmreich, *The German Churches Under Hitler* (Detroit: Wayne State University Press, 1979), 78–79.

In those areas where the German Christian ideology became ascendant, venerable Hebrew words like "hallelujah" and "amen" were deleted from the prayer books and hymnals, and all references to Jesus on the cross as "king of the Jews" were suppressed. See Salo Wittmayer Baron, *Modern Nationalism and Religion* (New York: Harper, 1947), 147.

[27]This ideology, also called free-enterprise capitalism, was enunciated by Adam Smith and Edmund Burke among others and is presently championed by George Gilder in his *Wealth and Poverty* (New York: Basic Books, 1981) and Irving Kristol in his *Two Cheers for Capitalism* (New York: Basic Books, 1978) and *Reflections of a Neoconservative* (New York: Basic Books, 1983). Burke declared: "The laws of commerce are the laws of nature and therefore the laws of God" (*Thoughts and Details on Scarcity* [1800], 31; cited in J. Wesley Bready, *England: Before and After Wesley* [London: Hodder & Stoughton, 1939], 126).

[28]Dietrich Bonhoeffer, *Ethics* Ed. Eberhard Bethge (New York: Macmillan, 1955), 103.

[29]Albert Camus, *The Myth of Sisyphus and Other Essays* Trans. Justin O'Brien (New York: Vintage Books, 1955), 80. Camus is here agreeing with Dostoevsky's character Kirilov and with Nietzsche.

[30]Cf. "The kingdom of grace has been conquered, but the kingdom of justice is crumbling too. Europe is dying of this disappointing realization." Albert Camus, *The Rebel*, Trans. Anthony Bower (New York: Knopf, 1961), 280.

CHAPTER FOUR–THE DARKENING HORIZON

[1]The introductory quotations from Nicholas Berdyaev in this book have been taken from his *The Fate of Man in the Modern World* (New York: Morehouse, 1935).

[2]For current insightful analyses of secular humanism see James Hitchcock, *What Is Secular Humanism?* (Ann Arbor: Servant Books, 1982); and Robert E. Webber, *Secular Humanism: Threat and Challenge* (Grand Rapids: Zondervan , 1982).

[3]Feodor Dostoevsky, *The Devils* trans. Constance Garnett, ed. Manuel Komroff (New York: New American Library, 1957), 573,588–89.

[4]Jacques Ellul, *Living Faith* trans. Peter Heinegg (San Francisco: Harper & Row, 1983), 51.

[5]Joseph Fletcher, situational ethicist, declares: "A fetus is a parasite, tolerable ethically only when welcome to its hostess. If a woman doesn't want a fetus to remain growing in her body, she should be free to rid herself of the unwelcome intruder." *National Catholic Reporter* 9 (March 2, 1973): 12.

[6]See Charles Hartshorne, "Concerning Abortion: an Attempt at a Rational View." *Christian Century* 98 (January 21, 1981): 42–45.

[7]See below, pp. 69–72

[8]T. V. Smith and Eduard Lindeman, *The Democratic Way of Life* (New York: New American Library, 1963), 19.

[9]See Ayn Rand, *The Virtue of Selfishness* (New York: New American Library, 1964). A similar position is taken by libertarian George H. Smith in his *Atheism: The Case Against God* (Los Angeles: Nash, 1974).

[10]Carl Oglesby, ed. *The New Left Reader* (New York: Grove, 1969), 265.

[11]For an incisive exposé of the pornography of power and the significant role of the Marquis de Sade in this abysmal aberration, see Rousas J. Rushdoony, *The Politics of Pornography* (New Rochelle, NY: Arlington House, 1974).

[12]*New York Times*, April 14, 1979, 5.

[13]*Christianity Today* 27 (November 25, 1983): 36.

[14]The Christian doctrine that all people are sinners was criticized by a Ministry of Culture spokesman in East Germany as being "a negation of the optimistic basis of socialist society" (*Christianity Today* 19 [October 25, 1974]: 45. More recently there has been an uneasy rapprochement between church and state in East Germany.

[15]The Marxist leadership of that country is now trying to force priests into the progovernment Catholic organization *Pacem in Terris* (Peace on Earth) whose purpose is to foster allegiance to the state. *Chicago Tribune*, July 2, 1983, Midwest Edition, sec. 1, p. 5. For information on an underground Catholic church in Slovakia, see Trevor Beeson, *Discretion and Valour: Religious Conditions in Russia and Eastern Europe* (Philadelphia: Fortress, 1982), 254.

[16]Roland Huntford, *The New Totalitarians* (New York: Stein & Day, 1972), 177.

[17]*Pulpit Helps* 8 (December 1982): 26.

[18]*World Christian* 2 (March-April 1983): 23.

[19]*Des Moines Register*, Nov. 3, 1983, 11A; cf. *Time* (July 23, 1984):61

[20]See especially "Ethiopia: Where Life Becomes Ever Harder," *British Weekly and Christian Record*, no. 5009 (May 6, 1983): 6. The report documents that Christians are frequently intimidated, and many are tortured, in a land where prison has become a way of life for God's people.

[21]To be sure, Proverbs 22:4 suggests that honor and prosperity will often follow humility, but the impression that the evangelist gave (perhaps this was not his intention) was that we should seek humility in order to have honor and prosperity. The New English Bible puts it this way: "The fruit of humility is the fear of God with riches and honour and life." The same chapter of Proverbs warns against trying to increase one's wealth at the expense of the poor (22:16).

[22]*New York Times*, July 1, 1974, 1, 20.

[23]*Christianity Today* 16 (February 18, 1972): 27.

[24]See Richard A. Baer, Jr., "A Critique of the Use of Values Clarification in Environmental Education," *The Journal of Environmental Education* 12 (Fall, 1980): 13–16; Richard A. Baer, Jr. "Values Clarification as Indoctrination," *The Educational Forum* 41 (January 1977): 155–65; Richard A. Baer Jr., "Parents, Schools and Values Clarification," *Wall Street Journal*, April 12, 1982, 22; and Alan L. Lockwood, "Values Education and the Right to Privacy," *Journal of Moral Education*, vol. 7, no. 1, 9–26.

[25]Belden Menkus, "Evangelical Responsibility in Public Education," *Christianity Today* 15 (February 12, 1971): 11; this is Menkus's interpretation of Ballinger's position. For an illuminating treatment of totalitarian tendencies in American education, see Rousas Rushdoony, *The Messianic Character of American Education* (Nutley, N.J.: Craig Press, 1968).

[26]John J. Dunphy, "A Religion for a New Age," *The Humanist* 43 (January-February 1983): 26.

[27]Arnold Beichman, "Have American Universities Forsaken Quest For Truth?," *Des Moines Sunday Register*, November 6, 1983, sec. C, 1, 3.

[28]*Christianity Today* 17 (February 16, 1973): 49. This would probably not happen today because of the outcome of the *Widmar v. Vincent* case. See "Text of the U. S. Supreme Court Decision: *Widmar v. Vincent*," *Journal of Church and State* 24 (Spring 1982): 433–42.

[29]*National Catholic Reporter* 7 (March 19, 1971): 1, 7.

[30]James Hitchcock, *The Decline and Fall of Radical Catholicism* (N.Y.: Herder & Herder, 1971), 194.

[31]Mark Branson, "Fundamentalism—Left and Right," *TSF Bulletin* 5 (May-June 1982): 2–3.

[32]Mother Basilea Schlink, *World in Revolt* (Minneapolis: Bethany, 1969), 5–6.

[33]The emphasis in the new social activism is on peace, women's liberation and the struggles of Third World peoples for economic and political independence.

[34]See e.g., Roger Corless, *The Art of Christian Alchemy: Transfiguring the Ordinary Through Holistic Meditation* (New York: Paulist, 1981). The author blends Eastern, medieval and Teilhardian insights.

[35]While process theology admittedly sees the need for an overarching metaphysical vision, it is pursued at the price of denying the reality of the supernatural. The only transcendence that is affirmed is a transcendence within immanence. By giving priority to becoming over being, process thought is admirably suited to the technological milieu. It should be noted that the schools of philosophy in most American and British universities are dominated not by process philosophy but by language analysis, which is antimetaphysical.

CHAPTER FIVE–THE MAIN THREATS TODAY

[1]See Jacques Ellul, *The Technological Society*, trans. John Wilkinson (New York: Vintage, 1964); *The Political Illusion*, trans. Konrad

Kellen (New York: Knopf, 1967); *False Presence of the Kingdom*, trans. C. Edward Hopkin (New York: Seabury, 1972); *The New Demons*, trans. C. Edward Hopkin (New York: Seabury, 1975); *The Betrayal of the West*, trans. Matthew J. O'Connell (New York: Seabury, 1978); and *Living Faith*, trans. Peter Heinegg (San Francisco: Harper & Row, 1983). These books form only a part of the Ellul corpus now in English.

[2]Where my critique of modern society is inclined to differ from Ellul's is that I see the pseudo-god of technology slowly but surely being edged out by the mystical gods and goddesses of the earth, blood and nation. Technological rationalism is being supplanted by a neomysticism that celebrates immersion in the world. It was Nietzsche, not Teilhard de Chardin or Marx, who correctly foresaw the new religious and cultural situation.

[3]A similar emphasis on the sacred character of creativity can be detected in Romanticism, but it was the creativity of artistic expression and spiritual insight rather than of technical accomplishment.

[4]Teilhard declared: "To what extent should not the development of the strong . . . take precedence over the preservation of the weak? How can we reconcile, in a state of maximum efficiency, the care lavished on the wounded with the more urgent necessities of battle?" Teilhard de Chardin, *Human Energy*, trans. J. M. Cohen (New York: Harcourt Brace Jovanovich, 1969), 133.

[5]Paul Vitz, *Psychology as Religion: The Cult of Self-Worship* (Grand Rapids: Eerdmans, 1977), 114.

[6]See William H. Whyte, Jr., *The Organization Man* (New York: Simon and Schuster, 1956).

[7]See Alvin Toffler, *Future Shock* (New York: Random House, 1970), 134–35. Toffler sees cultural pressures for decentralization and diversification and the eventual breakup of industrial hierarchy. Bureaucracy will give way to ad-hocracy, the fast-moving kinetic organization of the future.

In a more recent study, *The Third Wave* (New York: Bantam, 1982), Toffler entertains the semi-utopian vision of a new civilization emerging in which diversity rather than uniformity will characterize social life. He sees the disintegration of the traditional family structure as a sign of hope because it prepares the way for a new pattern of family organization that values human freedom and diversity. Toffler underestimates pressures for a new kind of conformity in the shift toward a commuter society. While not unaware of the lurking dangers of "electronic fascism" and "racial fanaticism," he is blithely confident that these can be overcome through human ingenuity.

Reflecting similar concerns, John Naisbitt in his *Megatrends* (New York: Warner Books, 1982), contends that industrial and managerial hierarchies are being supplanted by networks in which decisions are made by voluntary associations rather than corporate executives. We are moving, he says, from an industrial society to an information society, in which the economy is based more and more on an integrated communication system. He applauds what he believes to be a trend toward participatory over representative democracy and even participatory corporations as well as a rebirth of the spirit of the entrepreneur. The leaders of the future will be facilitators rather than bosses who issue orders. Social planners are still necessary, but they will achieve their objectives by consultation, feedback mechanisms and communication skills rather than by dictation or overt manipulation. States and regional bodies, moreover, will assume more and more responsibility for social planning. The author's ideological bias is evident in his defense of capitalism as the best means to advance the technological revolution.

In stark contrast to Ellul, both Toffler and Naisbitt regard high technology as a liberator rather than an enslaver of humankind. They see hope in a neopopulism, but what they fail to consider is that neopopulism is often the seedbed of nationalism. Interestingly, Naisbitt foresees "a renaissance in cultural and linguistic assertiveness" as nations become more dependent on one another economically (p. 76).

[8]Robert C. Harvey, *The Restless Heart* (Grand Rapids: Eerdmans, 1973).

[9]Ernst L. Freud, ed. *Letters of Sigmund Freud* (London: Hogarth, 1961), 432.

[10]Karl Stern tells of a conscientious objector who had been picked up as a psychiatric case in one of the medical wards where he had been admitted for a stomach ailment. (This was just after the Nazi seizure of power in Germany). He confided to the psychiatrist professor at the clinic that while serving in the trenches in the First World War, it suddenly dawned on him that killing was wrong. He had then resolved to devote his life to prayer and good works. After hearing this, the head psychiatrist diagnosed him as a schizophrenic, which meant that not only was he insane but also subject to compulsory sterilization. There was never any discussion. See Karl Stern, *The Pillar of Fire* (New York: Harcourt, Brace, 1951), 127–28.

[11]Thomas S. Szasz, *The Myth of Mental Illness* (New York: Harper & Row, 1974). See also his *The Manufacture of Madness* (New York: Harper & Row, 1970); and Martin L. Gross, *The Psychological Society* (New York: Random House, 1978).

[12]In Janice A. Broun, "A Soviet Cure for Religion," *America* 137 (July 16–23, 1977); 26–29. See also Zhores and Roy Medvedev, *A Question of Madness* (New York: Knopf, 1971).

[13]Hubert H. Humphrey, *The Cause is Mankind* (New York: Praeger, 1964), 98. For an illuminating commentary on this, see Rousas J. Rushdoony, *Politics of Guilt and Pity* (Nutley, NJ: Craig Press, 1970), 348.

[14]John Vinocur documents an emerging democratic totalitarianism in Socialist Sweden, bordering on an incipient fascism. He maintains that George Orwell's "1984" and Aldous Huxley's "Brave New World" are slowly becoming realities in modern Sweden. John Vinocur, "Is Tax Collector Becoming Sweden's Big Brother?," *Des Moines Register,* December 15, 1983, 15A. See also Roland Huntford, *The New Totalitarians* (New York: Stein & Day, 1972); Tom G. A. Hardt, "Sweden's War on the Family," *Christianity Today* 16 (July 7, 1972): 36–37; and Ami Lonnroth, "Current of Inequality That Runs Through Sweden's 'Feminist Utopia,'" *Des Moines Register,* March 19, 1980, 13A.

[15]Jean-Jacques Rousseau, who upheld the sovereignty of the general will, and John Dewey, who saw teachers as social servants dedicated to

maintaining social order, have both played a significant role in the shaping of totalitarian democracy. The consensualism of Carl Rogers should also be included as a factor in the emerging democratic collectivism.

According to Lester Crocker, for Rousseau "education" did not mean instruction but training for "docility," making people manageable by determining their behavior. See Lester G. Crocker, *Rousseau's Social Contract* (Cleveland: Press of Case Western Reserve University, 1968), 10.

For an incisive critique of the totalitarian bent of modern "democratic" education, see Rousas J. Rushdoony, *The Messianic Character of American Education* (Nutley, N.J.: Craig Press, 1968).

[16]B. F. Skinner, *Beyond Freedom and Dignity* (New York: Bantam Books, 1972).

[17]Jacques Ellul, *The Technological Society*, 375.

[18]*Commentary* 52 (August 1971): 8. The editor specifically has in mind those "progressive" forces that press for replacing the merit system in civil-service employment and in university admissions by a system of proportional representation based on race or ethnic origin. This action would hurt Jews the most, because they excel in the academic and business worlds far out of proportion to their numbers.

[19]*Des Moines Register*, April 4, 1972, 2.

[20]It should be noted that feminists in the Jungian camp such as Helen Luke and Ann Belford Ulanov are quite emphatic that there are psychic as well as biological differences between the sexes. Luke declares: "The biological difference between man and woman is never a 'nothing but'; it is a fundamental difference, and it does not stop with the body but implies an equally fundamental difference of *psychic* nature. . . .One of the most frightening characteristics of our present *Zeitgeist* is the urge to destroy difference, to reduce everything to a horrible sameness in the cause of 'equality'." (Helen M. Luke, *Woman Earth and Spirit* [New York: Crossroad, 1981], 2–3).

In my book *Is the Bible Sexist?* (Westchester, Ill.: Crossway Books, 1982), I propose a biblical alternative to both feminism and patriarchalism. While not disregarding both biological and psychic differences between the sexes, I affirm the essential equality of man and woman in Christ.

[21]P. T. Forsyth, *The Principle of Authority*, 2nd ed. (London: Independent Press, 1952), 253.

[22]See Bertram Gross, *Friendly Fascism: The New Face of Power in America* (New York: M. Evans, 1980). According to Gross, the persuasion on which the corporate state relies invariably takes the form of covert manipulation. He also gives us the needed reminder that the broadening of the democratic base may actually legitimize the concentration of power in the hands of the few (see esp. pp. 349–54). Gross can be faulted for his failure to point out that the corporate state may well include big labor as well as big business in collusion with a strong centralized (if not omnivorous) government.

[23]See Richard J. Mouw, "Dutch Pillars," *Reformed Journal* 32 (May 1982): 2–3.

[24]Michael Foot, former head of the Labor Party, is a member of the National Secular Society, which is committed to countering Christian values in public life, especially in education; *Christian Century* 100 (June 8–15, 1983): 573.

[25]See "A New Right Raises its Voice," *Time* 114 (August 13, 1979): 31; and Marci McDonald "Le Nouveau Nazism: A Rightist Fashion From France," *Saturday Review* 7 (February 2, 1980): 13–16. On the resurgence of racism in all of Western Europe, see John Nielsen, "Rising Racism on the Continent," *Time* 123 (February 6, 1984): 40–45.

[26]See Amry Vandenbosch, "A Barmen Declaration in South Africa," *Reformed Journal* 33 (March 1983): 14–16. It is also interesting to note that Afrikaner charismatics generally become more rather than less socially aware. See Marjorie Hope and James Young, *The South African Churches in a Revolutionary Situation* (Maryknoll: Orbis, 1981), 181.

[27]See John W. DeGruchy and Charles Villa-Vicencio, eds., *Apartheid Is a Heresy* (Grand Rapids: Eerdmans, 1983); and G. D. Cloete, "A New Confession in South Africa," *Reformed Journal* 34 (May 1984): 20–23.

[28]The nihilistic slant of National Socialism is spelled out in Hermann Rauschning, *The Revolution of Nihilism: Warning to the West* (New York: Longmans, Green, 1939).

[29]Nietzsche held that nihilism entails not only a drastic negation of all traditional values but also a resolute affirmation of a world without God and a willingness to create new values. In his philosophy, nihilism in the sense of viewing life as meaningless without moral law and devoid of all values belongs to the decadence of the West. Nietzsche saw his mission as heralding the transvaluation of all values, breaking through to a vision of a morality beyond good and evil. This could be accomplished only through the heroic will to power exercised by an enlightened and courageous creative minority, willing to rise above mass opinion. I shall be using the term "nihilism" mainly (but not exclusively) in its negative sense. See Friedrich Nietzsche, *The Philosophy of Nietzsche* (New York: Modern Library, 1927); Arthur C. Danto, *Nietzsche as Philosopher* (New York: Columbia University Press, 1980); Martin Heidegger, *Nietzsche: Nihilism* trans. Frank A. Capuzzi and David Farrell Krell (San Francisco: Harper & Row, 1982); and William Hubben, *Dostoevsky, Kierkegaard, Nietzsche, and Kafka* (New York: Collier, 1979), 89ff. For the differences between Nietzsche and the earlier Russian nihilists, see the first chapter in Arthur Danto's book.

[30]The commandment of the living God seems to have as little impact on the secular peace movement as on the nihilistic right. Both movements see peace as resting on human ingenuity and sagacity rather than on divine intervention into history. The God of both the ideological right and the peace militants is at the most a deistic God who stands aloof from human affairs, leaving humanity to its own fate. These remarks do not pertain to those in the peace movement who are motivated by an earnest desire to bear witness to the Prince of Peace, Jesus Christ.

[31]In Herman Kahn's celebrated *On Thermonuclear War* (Princeton, N.J.: Princeton University Press, 1960), nowhere in the 651 pages are there any traces of ethical reservations or qualms of guilt.

[32]Jacques Ellul, *Living Faith*, 230. Ellul specifically has in mind "movements promoting homosexuality, radical feminism, and sexual freedom, or attacking the family and decency."

[33]Aleksandr I. Solzhenitsyn, *Letter to the Soviet Leaders*, trans. Hilary Sternberg (New York: Harper & Row, 1975), 52–53.

[34]Gregory Davis ably shows how the thrust of modern technology tends to the direction of a technological nihilism, in which there is a preoccupation with technological innovation coupled with a blithe indifference to effects. See Gregory H. Davis, *Technology—Humanism or Nihilism: A Critical Analysis of the Philosophical Basis and Practice of Modern Technology* (Washington, DC: University Press of America, 1981). Davis proposes a new kind of technological humanism, in which technology is subordinated to human welfare.

[35]On Tillich's discussion of this typology, see Paul Tillich, *The Protestant Era*, trans. James Luther Adams (Chicago: University of Chicago Press, 1948), xvi, 44–48, 55–61.

[36]Naomi Goldenberg, *Changing of the Gods* (Boston: Beacon Press, 1979). See also Margot Adler, *Drawing Down the Moon* (Boston: Beacon Press, 1979).

[37]An illuminating discussion of the pansexualism of Reich and Lawrence is to be found in Philip Rieff, *The Triumph of the Therapeutic* (N.Y.: Harper & Row, 1966). Both men, it seems, sought to return to the religion of the Earth Mother.

[38]This thesis is documented by Os Guinness in his *The Dust of Death* (Downers Grove: InterVarsity, 1973).

[39]It is to be noted that Nietzsche saw the coming aeon as a tragic age. For him, tragedy brings a "higher joy" that reconciles mystical and worldly instincts. See M. S. Silk and J. P. Stern, *Nietzsche on Tragedy* (Cambridge: Cambridge University Press, 1983), 285, 331. Also see Friedrich Nietzsche, *The Birth of Tragedy and the Case of Wagner*, ed. and trans. Walter Kaufmann (New York: Vintage Books, 1967).

[40]In the Romantic poet Lord Byron, we see the startling combination of Satanism and nationalism.

Ellul suggests that belief in the *diabolos* is present everywhere today but that it is hidden in our commitment to myths of sexuality, technology and politics. Jacques Ellul, *Living Faith*, see esp. pp. 61–68.

[41]Alvin Toffler has this report on a visit to Moscow: "Soviet anti-semitic persecution is known all over the world. But many Russians also hold nastily racist attitudes toward Moslems and other minorities. And in Moscow, we were repeatedly warned by Russians against the so-called 'yellow peril' posed by China." He goes on to tell of "outbreaks of racial and ethnic violence in the Red Army, in which the officers tend to be Russian, the noncoms Ukrainian, and the troops made up largely of other nationalities or racial groups." (Alvin Toffler, *Previews and Premises* [New York: William Morrow, 1983], 147–48).

[42]D. H. Lawrence voiced the new mood when he declared: "My great religion is a belief in the blood, the flesh, as being wiser than the intellect. We can go wrong with our minds, but what our blood feels and believes and says is always true. . . . The real way of living is to answer one's wants" (quoted in Arnold Lunn and Garth Lean, *The New Morality* [London: Blandford, 1964], 80). Cf.: "The blood-consciousness is the first and last knowledge of the living soul: the depths. . . . And blood-consciousness cannot operate purely until the soul has put off all its manifold degrees and forms of upper consciousness" (D. H. Lawrence, *Psychoanalysis and the Unconscious and Fantasia of the Unconscious* [New York: Viking, 1971], 202). Lawrence envisaged God as "the Cosmic Spirit" or "the Oversoul" (Edward D. McDonald, ed. *Phoenix: The Posthumous Papers of D. H. Lawrence* [New York: Viking, 1936]).

Lawrence's views are reflected in the Green Revolution, exemplified in the hippies and flower children of the 60s and in a growing number of the antiwar activists in Germany and other Western nations today. Lawrence, it should be noted, was fascinated with the gods of Greek mythology, Pan and Apollo, as well as with the Egyptian gods of fertility, Isis and Osiris. All of these deities bear a direct relation to nature mysticism.

A contemporary writer in tune with the spirit of the new age is Meinrad Craighead, who calls for a religion that "is connected to the metamorphoses of nature: the pure potential of water, the transformative power of blood, the seasonal rhythms of the earth, the cycles of lunar dark and light" (Meinrad Craighead, "Immanent Mother," in Mary E. Giles, ed. *The Feminist Mystic and Other Essays of Women and Spirituality* [New York: Crossroad, 1982], 79.

[43]Cf. Heraclitus: "War is the father of all and the king of all; and some he has made gods and some men, some bond and some free. . . . We must know that war is common to all and strife is justice, and that all things come into being and pass away through strife" (John Burnet, *Early Greek Philosophy,* 4th ed. [London: Adam & Charles Black, 1930], 136–37).

It is well to note that the way of violence is also championed by a growing number of militant feminists as an answer to male violence against women. Rosemary Ruether seeks to counter this kind of feminism in her "Feminism and Peace," *Christian Century* 100 (August 31-September 7, 1983): 771–76.

[44]From his *The Gay Science;* in Walter Kaufmann, ed. *Existentialism From Dostoevsky to Sartre,* Revised. (New York: New American Library, 1975), 127.

[45]Philosophers associated with a new this-worldly mysticism include William Blake, Friedrich Nietzsche, Friedrich W. Schelling, Friedrich Schleiermacher, Walt Whitman, Nikos Kazantzakis, Henri Bergson, Fritjof Capra, Teilhard de Chardin, D. H. Lawrence, Wilhelm Reich, Carl Jung, Martin Heidegger, Sri Aurobindo, Thomas Altizer, Matthew Fox, Alfred Rosenberg and Richard Rubenstein. This world-affirming mysticism is to be contrasted with the world-denying mysticism of Schopenhauer and Krishnamurti, heavily influenced by Indian religion and philosophy. It is also to be differentiated from classical Christian mysticism, which relativizes worldly endeavor. This last kind of mysticism, which has a

Neoplatonic cast, is represented in our time by Gerald Heard, Simone Weil, Evelyn Underhill, Thomas Merton and George Maloney.

In neomysticism, eternity is experienced in bodily sensations and the will to pleasure and power. In traditional forms of mysticism, eternity is experienced by rising above physical passion, by breaking free from the bonds of temporality and materiality.

[46]Alfred Rosenberg, the theorist of National Socialism, interestingly enough entitled his magnum opus *Der Mythus des 20. Jahrhunderts* [*The Myth of the Twentieth Century*] (München: Hoheneichen-Verlag, 1930). For an English translation of excerpts from Rosenberg's writings, see Robert Pois, ed. *Race and Race History and Other Essays* (New York: Harper & Row, 1970).

Rosenberg appeals to both Nietzsche and Meister Eckhart in support of his racialistic mysticism, but he has an uncanny ability to take both men out of context. Although Nietzsche's writings cannot be construed as anti-Semitic, his statements eulogizing the strong races of North Europe and his attack on Jewish-Christian morality were gladly exploited by Hitler's disciples.

The so-called New Age movement, with its curious blend of racism, occultism, and evolutionism, is a more recent expression of neopagan resurgence. Two key symbols in this movement are the rainbow and the swastika. While investigators of New Agism such as Constance Cumbey have made some questionable allegations, it cannot be doubted that the occultist writings of Alice Bailey and David Spangler are exerting an unwholesome influence on an increasing number of organizations—both cultural and religious. See Constance E. Cumbey, *The Hidden Dangers of the Rainbow* (Shreveport: Huntington House, 1983). In my opinion, Cumbey fails to present a convincing case for a monolithic New Age conspiracy. For a critical examination of some of her claims, see Randy Frame, "Is the Antichrist in the World Today?" *Christianity Today* 27 (September 2, 1983): 55–65. For a more balanced appraisal of this cult movement, showing how it often comes cloaked in the language of science and humanism, see Robert Burrows, "The New Age Movement," *Evangelical Newsletter* 11 (May 11, 1984): 3–4. Burrows maintains that the New Age movement "has as its goal individual and corporate deification."

[47]See Gerald A. Vanderhaar, *Christians and Nonviolence in the Nuclear Age* (Mystic, CT: Twenty-Third Publications, 1982), 35–36. The author notes that other weapon systems have carried such names as Thor, Atlas and Valkerie, all derived from mythological divinities. He also reminds us that the two key elements in nuclear weaponry, uranium and plutonium, are named after ancient pagan deities, the first after Uranus, the Greek sky god, and the second after Pluto, the Roman god of the underworld.

[48]I do not dispute the fact that the name of this submarine was taken from a city in Texas and not directly from the Bible or Christian liturgy. At the same time, it reveals in a startling way the frantic search in high circles for religious sanction for modern weaponry. Those who employ such seminal symbols as Atlas, Trident and Corpus Christi are often unaware or only remotely aware of their deeper implications.

CHAPTER SIX—THE CHURCH IN DISARRAY

[1]See Ralph Martin, _A Crisis of Truth_ (Ann Arbor, Mich.: Servant Books, 1982), 15.

[2]Kenneth Slack, "Depressing Statistics: English Church Life," _Christian Century_ 100 (November 16, 1983): 1038. Another study, conducted by the British Council of Churches, discloses that 71% of Britain's teenagers who had attended church at age 14 had left by the time they had reached the age of 20 (_Christianity Today_ 28 [June 15, 1984]: 66).

[3]_Christian Century_ 100 (June 22–29, 1983): 606.

[4]_Context_ 11 (August 15, 1979): 6.

[5]See Adolph Schalk, "The Church in France: Proud Vineyard, Poor Harvest," _U. S. Catholic_ 40 (June 1975): 19–24.; Alain Woodrow, "Post-Conciliar Catholicism: France in Search of a Destination," _Commonweal_ 98 (March 16, 1973): 31–35; "Crisis and Change in French Churches," _Christian Century_ 98 (June 3–10, 1981): 644–48.

[6]In _Christianity Today_ 27 (June 17, 1983): 54.

[7]Gwynne Dyer, "Has U. S. Become God's Last Country?" _Des Moines Register_, February 25, 1980, 7A.

[8]_Christianity Today_ 16 (July 7, 1972): 5.

[9]Especially ominous for Roman Catholicism in this country is the precipitous decline in religious vocations. In 1962, 48,000 young men entered Catholic seminaries for the purpose of priestly ordination; in 1983 the number had dropped to 12,054 (_Des Moines Register_, December 5, 1983, 20A). The statistics for sisterhoods are no less disconcerting. See _Time_ 122 (November 28, 1983): 95.

[10]Bruce Buursma, "Once Again, Religion Offers the Answers," _Chicago Tribune_, September 17, 1983, sec. 1, p. 6.

[11]Ibid. A more sobering appraisal of religion in America is also given by Pat Egan, a Roman Catholic priest-sociologist from London, England. His conclusion is that despite the broad interest in religion, America is steadily becoming more secularized. See his "Is America Becoming More Christian or Less?" _Pastoral Renewal_ 8 (March 1984): 104–7.

[12]_National Review_ 35 (April 15, 1983): 429.

[13]See David Gelman with B. K. Gangelhoff, "Teen-age Suicide in the Sun Belt," _Newsweek_ 102 (August 15, 1983): 70–74.

[14]Michael Novak, "The Religious Consciousness of the Professional-Managerial Class," _Christian Century_ 93 (March 10, 1976): 217–24.

[15]_National Catholic Reporter_ 9 (January 26, 1973): 6.

[16]On recent Baptist gains in Russia, see "Baptists in Russia Look Back on Significant Church Growth," _British Weekly and Christian Record_, no. 5010 (May 13, 1983), 3.

[17]See Jacques Ellul, _Violence_, trans. Cecelia Gaul Kings (New York: Seabury, 1969).

[18]P. T. Forsyth, _Positive Preaching and the Modern Mind_ (London: Independent Press, 1953), 133.

[19]Vernard Eller, ed. *Thy Kingdom Come: A Blumhardt Reader* (Grand Rapids: Eerdmans, 1980), 69.

[20]"A Bleak Outlook is Seen for Religion," *New York Times*, February 25, 1968, 3.

[21]Martin Smith, "Christianity Re-Judaizes," *National Catholic Reporter* 13 (December 24, 1976): 8.

[22]James Davison Hunter, *American Evangelicalism* (New Brunswick, NJ: Rutgers University Press, 1983), 122–23. Hunter's criticisms pertain mainly to that segment of evangelicalism influenced by the New Thought movement. In these circles, the Bible is important because it gives us the principles that enable us to live successful lives. The penetration of New Thought in modern evangelicalism is amply documented by Richard Quebedeaux in his *By What Authority* (San Francisco: Harper & Row, 1982).

[23]Cf. Dietrich von Hildebrand, *Trojan Horse in the City of God* (Chicago: Franciscan Herald, 1967); Louis Bouyer, *The Decomposition of Catholicism* (Chicago: Franciscan Herald, 1969); and Ralph Martin, *A Crisis of Truth* (Ann Arbor: Servant Books, 1982).

[24]For a welcome critique of this position see Avery Dulles, *Models of Revelation* (New York: Doubleday, 1983), 98–114, 152–54. At certain points, Dulles shows that he himself is vulnerable to the unwise speculations of the new Catholicism. See my review of his book in *Christian Century* 100 (November 16, 1983): 1057–58.

[25]See José Miranda, *Communism in the Bible*, trans. Robert Barr (New York: Orbis, 1982).

CHAPTER SEVEN—NEW MODELS FOR THE CHURCH

[1]See E. H. Robertson, *Paul Schneider: The Pastor of Buchenwald* (Chicago: SCM Book Club, 1956).

[2]See Eberhard Bethge, *Dietrich Bonhoeffer*, ed. Edwin Robertson, trans. Eric Mosbacher, Peter and Betty Ross, Frank Clarke and William Glen-Doepel (New York: Harper & Row, 1970); and Mary Bosanquet, *The Life and Death of Dietrich Bonhoeffer* (New York: Harper & Row, 1968).

[3]See Corrie ten Boom with John and Elizabeth Sherrill, *The Hiding Place* (Carmel, NY: Guideposts, 1971); Corrie ten Boom, *He Sets the Captive Free* (Old Tappan, NJ: Revell, 1977); and *Corrie ten Boom's Prison Letters* (Old Tappan, NJ: Revell, 1975).

[4]See Gordon C. Zahn, *In Solitary Witness: The Life and Death of Franz Jägerstätter* (New York: Holt, Rinehart & Winston, 1964).

[5]Zahn nonetheless documents a pacifist bent in Jägerstätter. See Ibid., 129–32.

[6]See Richard Wurmbrand, *Christ in the Communist Prisons*, ed. Charles Foley (New York: Coward-McCann, 1968); Richard Wurmbrand, *Sermons in Solitary Confinement* (London: Hodder & Stoughton, 1969); and Mary Drewer, *Richard Wurmbrand: The Man Who Came Back* (London: Hodder & Stoughton, 1974).

[7]See Janice A. Broun, "Evangelism in the U.S.S.R.," *Christianity Today*," 18 *(June 21, 1974): 13.*

[8]See Trevor Beeson, "Martyrdom in Albania," *Christian Century* 90 (September 26, 1973): 958

[9]See József Cardinal Mindszenty, *Memoirs* (New York: Macmillan, 1974); and *Cardinal Mindszenty Speaks* (New York: Longmans, Green and Co., 1949).

[10]See Russell T. Hitt, *Jungle Pilot: The Life and Witness of Nate Saint* (New York, Harper & Bros., 1959).

[11]See Carl Philip Anderson, *There Was a Man, His Name: Paul Carlson* (Westwood, NJ: Revell, 1965); and Lois Carlson, *Monganga Paul: The Congo Ministry and Martyrdom of Paul Carlson, M.D.* (New York: Harper & Row, 1966).

[12]See Georgi Vins, *Georgi Vins: Prisoner of Conscience*, trans. Jane Ellis (Elgin: David C. Cook, 1975); and Wayne A. Detzler, *The Changing Church in Europe* (Grand Rapids: Zondervan, 1979), 137–39, 162, 216.

[13]See Alexander Schmemann, "On Alexander Solzhenitsyn" in John B. Dunlop, Richard Haugh, and Alexis Klimoff, *Aleksandr Solzhenitsyn: Critical Essays and Documentary Materials* (Belmont, MA: Nordland, 1973), 28-44; and Edward E. Ericson, Jr., *Solzhenitsyn: The Moral Vision* (Grand Rapids: Eerdmans, 1980).

[14]Bishop Tutu is adamant that "it is not politics" but "the Gospel of Jesus Christ" that "will set us free." While sympathetic to the concerns of liberation theology, he questions the wisdom of letting the world set the agenda for the church: "What I am trying to underline is that we cannot denigrate the Church, and devalue it, because we want to enhance the value of the world. . . .Let us be the Church of God, fearlessly proclaiming the Gospel" (Desmond Tutu, *Crying in the Wilderness*, ed. John Webster [Grand Rapids: Eerdmans, 1982], 32, 35–36).

Bishop Tutu is not only blessed with a deep social conscience that has led him to identify with the struggle of oppressed peoples for liberation but is also a man of piety, frequently spending several hours a day in prayer; see Marjorie Hope and James Young, *The South African Churches in a Revolutionary Situation* (Maryknoll: Orbis, 1981), 109-15.

CHAPTER EIGHT—THE CHALLENGE FACING CHURCHES AND SEMINARIES

[1]Cited in Eberhard Busch, *Karl Barth: His Life from Letters and Autobiographical Texts*, trans. John Bowden (Philadelphia: Fortress, 1976), 375.

[2]P. T. Forsyth, *The Church and the Sacraments* (London: Independent Press, 1947), 35.

[3]Nevertheless, I believe that evangelicalism as an ideal type of Christianity grounded in and committed to the proclamation of the gospel is reflected to a greater degree in the popular movements that bear the name "evangelical" than in such denominations as the United Church of Christ, the United Methodist Church and the Disciples of Christ, where

the focus is on the humanizing of culture rather than the conversion of a lost world to the gospel.

[4]Bernard Ramm, *After Fundamentalism: The Future of Evangelical Theology* (San Francisco: Harper & Row, 1983), 50–51.

[5]Edward Farley, *Theologia: The Fragmentation and Unity of Theological Education* (Philadelphia: Fortress, 1983), 43.

[6]Jacques Ellul, *Living Faith,* trans. Peter Heinegg (San Francisco: Harper & Row, 1983), 123.

[7]A church can afford to tolerate a certain degree of heterodoxy, i.e., an imbalance in the presentation of the faith, but it can ill afford to tolerate heresy, an attack on the vitals of the faith, especially when this heresy is openly promulgated from the pulpits of the church.

[8]See Robert Brinsmead, "The Gospel versus the Sectarian Spirit," *Verdict* 4 (March 1981), 8–16.

[9]For a further discussion of the differences between Tillich and Barth, see Donald G. Bloesch, *The Ground of Certainty* (Grand Rapids: Eerdmans, 1971), 42–50. Also see Donald G. Bloesch, *The Christian Witness in a Secular Age* (Minneapolis: Augsburg, 1968), ch. 3 and 7.

[10]Tillich's theological methodology is spelled out in his *Systematic Theology,* vol. 1 (Chicago: University of Chicago Press, 1951). See especially pp. 30–34, 59–60, 64–66. Also see James Luther Adams, *Paul Tillich's Philosophy of Culture, Science, and Religion* (New York: Harper & Row, 1965).

[11]See Friedrich Schleiermacher, *On Religion: Speeches to its Cultured Despisers,* trans. John Oman, introduction by Rudolf Otto (New York: Harper Torchbooks, 1958).

[12]For relevant works of Reinhold Niebuhr, see his *The Nature and Destiny of Man,* 2 vols. (New York: Scribner's, 1951); *Faith and History* (New York: Scribner's, 1949); and *The Self and the Dramas of History* (New York: Scribner's, 1955). For pertinent books by Emil Brunner, see his *Revelation and Reason,* trans. Olive Wyon (Philadelphia: Westminster, 1946); and *The Christian Doctrine of God,* trans. Olive Wyon (Philadelphia: Westminster, 1950).

[13]See H. Richard Niebuhr, *Christ and Culture* (New York: Harper & Bros., 1951).

[14]This means that in an age of growing laxity in areas of sexuality the church should uphold holy virginity and holy marriage as the only permissible options for the Christian. The call to chastity should again be sounded, and celibacy for the sake of the kingdom should be treated as a live alternative to marriage in the Lord.

CHAPTER NINE—HUMAN FOLLY AND DIVINE GRACE

[1]Both theologians and cultural analysts after World War II frequently made the distinction between D Day, the day of decision when the troops of America and Britain landed in Normandy, thus virtually sealing Hitler's doom, and V Day, the day of final victory, when the German state unconditionally surrendered to the allied forces.

[2]That the vision of the apocalypse is by no means foreign to contemporary culture is documented in J. Christiaan Beker, *Paul's Apocalyptic Gospel* (Philadelphia: Fortress, 1982). He sees no need to contrast the apocalyptic with the scientific world view.

[3]Francis Schaeffer states the case for civil disobedience on the part of Christians besieged by a secular culture. Francis A. Schaeffer, *A Christian Manifesto* (Westchester, IL: Crossway, 1981). My principal objection to Schaeffer is that he allows for taking up arms in defense of the kingdom of God. The church of the Reformation permitted the sword as necessary for the maintenance of public order but never as a means to defend or advance the kingdom of Christ, which is not of this world.

[4]Vernard Eller, ed. *Thy Kingdom Come: A Blumhardt Reader* (Grand Rapids: Eerdmans, 1980), 84.

[5]Ibid.

CHAPTER TEN—DISCIPLESHIP UNDER THE CROSS

[1]The paradox of inward detachment from the claims of the world and passionate involvement in its fundamental questions is succinctly stated by Jacques Ellul: "We must break off and leave them [those who belong to the world], so that they can hear that strange word of God which cannot be uttered except both at the center and from an infinite distance. The point is not to break off the dialog or to retire to the desert, but the word of God can be proclaimed only by someone who places himself outside 'the world,' while staying at the very heart of the questioning that goes on within it." Jacques Ellul, *Living Faith* (San Francisco: Harper & Row, 1983), 277.

[2]Cited by Norman Pittenger, *After Death—Life in God* (New York: Seabury, 1980), 38.

[3]Ellul incisively observes that humanitarian works if done without God will end in accomplishing the opposite of what was intended. The reason is that "at the heart of such works, even the best of them, lies coiled the serpent of human perversion and degradation." Ellul, *Living Faith*, 256–57.

[4]Cf. Barth: "The kingdom of God does not begin with our movements of protest. It is the revolution which is before all revolutions, as it is before the whole prevailing order of things." (*The Word of God and the Word of Man*, trans. Douglas Horton [Gloucester, MA: Peter Smith, 1978], 299.

[5]This is not to deny that political or social reforms that proceed out of the imperatives of the gospel can prepare the way for the kingdom by removing obstacles to the hearing and obeying of the gospel. But these kinds of reforms can take place only when the Spirit is at work creating a yearning for the spiritual righteousness of the kingdom. Social reform in and of itself cannot contribute in the slightest to the new horizon of meaning symbolized by the kingdom of God. But when social reform is informed by and united with the gospel proclamation, it can serve to remind people of the claims of a higher law than civil law and a higher righteousness than civil righteousness.

Scripture Index

Name Index

Subject Index